AI WEALTH ENTREPRENEUR

HOW ANYONE CAN MAKE MONEY ONLINE WITH ARTIFICIAL INTELLIGENCE IN JUST 30 MINUTES A DAY

MONIKA ALI KHAN PHD

LIGHTHOUSE SHINE PUBLISHING

consultation. The information herein has been compiled from various sources, and readers are encouraged to consult licensed professionals before implementing any practices outlined in this book.

Before undertaking any investment, it is essential to seek advice from a financial advisor and consider the investment's objectives, risks, fees, and expenses thoroughly. Past performance does not guarantee future results.

By proceeding with this material, the reader agrees to the stipulated terms, acknowledging the educational and entertainment purpose of the document and assuming full responsibility for any outcomes derived from its use.

Editor, Cover and Interior Designed by Lighthouse Shine Publishing.

www.LighthouseShinePublishing.com

———

Scan this QR code or visit https://aiwealthentrepreneur.com/tools for AI 100+ Toolkit and updates to this book.

CONTENTS

INTRODUCTION

From Scientist to Creator: My Journey into AI

As a scientist, my days were filled with research, data analysis, and experiments. The structured and logical nature of my work was satisfying, but a part of me craved something more—a creative outlet to balance the strictness of scientific work. I always dreamed of creating digital art and writing books, but the demands of my career left little time for these passions.

Then, in December 2022, everything changed. I found an article about the growing field of artificial intelligence (AI) and its use in creative projects. Curious, I enrolled in some beginner courses to explore this new area. What started as a simple curiosity quickly became a profound journey. Over the next year and a half, I learned AI, completed several courses, and mastered various AI tools from home.

This journey not only reignited my creative passions but also revealed AI's endless possibilities.

Incorporating AI into my work has also shown me that AI is not about replacing humans with robots. Instead, it's about enhancing our capabilities and expanding the horizons of what we can achieve. AI can handle repetitive tasks, analyze large datasets, and even suggest new research directions, allowing scientists to focus on more complex and innovative aspects of their work. The teamwork between AI and human intelligence leads to new progress in science and creativity.

AI: The Bridge Between Science and Creativity

AI has transformed from a complex, enigmatic technology into a versatile tool accessible to everyone. For me, it became the bridge between my scientific background and my creative aspirations. This book, "AI Wealth Entrepreneur: How Anyone Can Make Money Online with Artificial Intelligence in Just 30 Minutes a Day," is the culmination of my AI journey so far, blending my scientific background with my revived creative passions. It is designed to guide you through leveraging AI to create multiple streams of income, regardless of your prior knowledge or technical skills.

Universal Appeal: Crafted for Absolute Beginners

Whether you're a scientist, an artist, or someone who is simply curious about the potential of AI, this book is for you. You don't need to be a tech expert to benefit from it. I was once a beginner too, navigating the complexities of AI. That's why this guide is tailored for absolute beginners, offering a clear, step-by-step path to mastering AI tools and creating income streams. You can become an AI Wealth Entrepreneur. The AI revolution will transform millionaires into billionaires and billionaires into trillionaires. Are you ready to propel your business into the new trillion-dollar AI economy?

A Compelling Book Structure

Here's what you can expect as you journey through this book:

1. **Getting Started with AI**: Demystifying AI and showing you how to set up your first AI-powered income stream.
2. **Step-by-Step Guides**: Detailed tutorials on various AI tools (such as ChatGPT) and platforms, making implementation a breeze.
3. **Real-Life Success Stories**: Inspiring tales of individuals who have successfully harnessed AI to achieve financial independence.
4. **Actionable Advice**: Practical tips and strategies to maximize your earnings and sustain long-term growth.

Realistic Expectations: Patience and Dedication Required

While AI presents immense opportunities, it's important to set realistic expectations. Success doesn't happen overnight. It requires patience, dedication, and a willingness to learn and adapt. This book will provide you with the knowledge and tools, but your dedication will determine your success.

Ethical AI Use: A Responsibility

In embracing AI, we must also consider its ethical implications. Using AI responsibly ensures that we contribute positively to society and build trust in this transformative technology. Throughout this book, I will emphasize ethical practices, helping you navigate the moral landscape of AI use.

> "Artificial Intelligence is the new electricity. Just as electricity transformed industries 100 years ago, AI will transform our world today."
>
> ANDREW NG

This quote encapsulates the spirit of this book—AI is a powerful force for change, and with the right knowledge and approach, it can transform your financial life.

I invite you to embark on this journey with an open mind and a proactive attitude. The path to financial growth through AI is filled with learning and discovery, and I am here to guide you every step of the way. Together, we will unlock AI's potential and achieve financial freedom.

It's natural to have fears and misconceptions about AI. You might worry that it's too complicated or that it's a passing trend. Rest assured, this book will demystify AI and show you how accessible and beneficial it can be. AI is here to stay, and it's transforming lives—let it transform yours too.

Hundreds of AI tools are released every day, and my team and I are always testing them to stay on top of the best, most money-making AI tools as they are released. This resource is perfect for everyone from marketers to students, content creators, coaches, consultants, busy parents, and business owners, providing tools to help you learn, create, and earn more than ever with ChatGPT and its companion tools. Whether you're a beginner or an enthusiast, this book will guide you in discovering new ideas and sources of future AI passive income without straining your budget.

To get our specially selected AI 100+ Toolkit, go to:
   https://aiwealthentrepreneur.com/tools
   or scan the QR code below.

With passion and dedication, I am excited to share this journey with you. Let's explore the incredible potential of AI in creating a future of financial freedom and empowerment.

CHAPTER 1
DEMYSTIFYING AI FOR BEGINNERS

1.1 THE BASICS OF AI: A BEGINNER'S GUIDE

efinition and Scope
Artificial Intelligence, or AI, refers to computer systems performing tasks that typically require human intelligence. These tasks include learning, reasoning, problem-solving, understanding natural language, and perceiving environments. The scope of AI spans from simple algorithms capable of specific tasks to advanced systems able to make complex decisions.

Evolution of AI

The journey of AI began with basic algorithms and has since evolved into advanced neural networks that mimic human cognitive functions. In the early days, AI consisted of rule-based systems that could perform specific tasks, like solving mathematical problems. The development of machine learning algorithms enables systems to learn from data and improve performance over time without explicit programming. Today, deep learning and neural networks have taken AI to new heights, allowing machines to recognize patterns, understand speech, and even generate human-like text.

Types of AI

AI can be categorized into three main types:

- **Narrow AI**: Also known as weak AI, this type is designed to perform a specific task, such as facial recognition or language translation. Narrow AI is prevalent in today's applications and does not possess general intelligence.
- **General AI**: Also referred to as strong AI, general AI can understand, learn, and apply knowledge across a wide range of tasks, similar to human intelligence. This level of AI is still theoretical and has not yet been achieved.
- **Superintelligent AI**: This concept involves AI that surpasses human intelligence in all aspects, including creativity and problem-solving. Superintelligent AI remains a topic of speculation and ethical debate.

Examples of AI Tools:

One notable tool is **Grammarly**, an AI-powered writing assistant that not only corrects grammatical errors but also improves style and clarity. For those involved in graphic design, **Canva** utilizes AI to suggest design elements and layouts, making professional-quality design accessible to everyone. In the realm of customer service, **ChatGPT** provides sophisticated conversational capabilities, enabling businesses to automate and enhance their customer interactions with human-like dialogue. **Jasper** is another impressive AI tool, generating high-quality marketing copy and content ideas tailored to specific audiences. Additionally, **DALL-E** leverages AI to create detailed and imaginative images from textual descriptions, opening new avenues for creative expression. These tools, among others, demonstrate the profound impact of AI on various industries, streamlining processes and fostering innovation.

AI has the ability to revolutionize business processes and automate and optimize them. This can be seen across different domains, where various tools exemplify the transformative power of AI. For further details on how AI can be leveraged for financial independence and beyond, exploring these tools and their applications is an insightful start.

1.2 UNDERSTANDING MACHINE LEARNING: THE BRAIN BEHIND AI

Fundamentals of Machine Learning:

Machine learning is the foundation of modern artificial intelligence, allowing machines to learn and enhance their performance through data without explicit programming. It's crucial to grasp these core concepts to understand AI's capabilities and limitations. Microsoft's training material on machine learning fundamentals is a valuable resource that covers the basics, different types, and considerations for training and evaluating models, including deep learning and automated machine learning applications.

Supervised vs. Unsupervised Learning

The landscape of machine learning is broadly categorized into supervised and unsupervised learning. In supervised learning, a function connects an input with an output based on given input-output pairs. Unsupervised learning discovers hidden patterns in input data. Understanding these two types' distinctions is critical for applying the right approach to various AI problems.

Real-World Applications

Machine learning applications are ubiquitous, transforming industries by enhancing recommendation systems, enabling sophisticated fraud detection mechanisms, and more. These real-world applications underscore machine learning technologies' practical value and transformative potential in daily life.

Machine Learning and Financial Growth

The financial growth opportunities machine learning presents are vast, ranging from predictive analytics in stock markets to personalized financial advice and fraud prevention. Machine learning's ability to analyze large datasets and uncover insights can lead to better decision-making and new income-generating avenues.

The fundamentals of machine learning include a variety of concepts and techniques, such as cross-validation methods like Leave One Out Cross Validation (LOOCV) and K-fold Cross Validation, which are essential for developing robust machine learning models. Moreover, bootstrapping and optimization techniques, such as hyperparameter optimization, enhance model performance and accuracy.

By understanding these essential aspects, individuals and businesses can leverage machine learning to unlock new possibilities for innovation and financial growth.

1.3 DECODING AI JARGON: A GLOSSARY OF ESSENTIAL TERMS

Key Terminologies Explained

Artificial Intelligence (AI) spans a broad spectrum of concepts and technologies that can often seem daunting to beginners. Key terms include:

- **Algorithm**: A finite set of instructions followed by a computer system to perform tasks.
- **Machine Learning (ML)**: Utilizes algorithms that learn from data to enhance their performance, allowing computers to tackle complex problems and tasks beyond human manual capabilities.
- **Deep Learning**: A subset of ML based on artificial neural networks, mimicking the human brain's structure and function.
- **Natural Language Processing (NLP)**: The technology behind how computers understand and process human language.
- **Neural Networks**: Are computer systems designed to imitate the human brain's neuron network, playing a pivotal role in advancing deep learning technologies.

Contextualizing AI Terms in Business

Understanding these terms is not just academic; it has practical business implications. For example:

- **Big Data**: Datasets of considerable size that can be analyzed through computational methods to identify patterns, trends, and associations, particularly those related to human behavior and interactions. It's pivotal in making informed business decisions.

- **Generative AI**: AI that can generate new content, such as text, images, or music, has immense applications in marketing, entertainment, and personalized customer experiences.

Importance of Understanding AI Lingo

Grasping AI terminology is crucial for several reasons:

- It facilitates effective communication with tech teams and stakeholders.
- Understanding these terms allows a better assessment of AI's potential impact and limitations within your business context.
- It empowers you to stay informed about the latest advancements and their applications.

Resources for Further Learning

Numerous resources are available for deepening your understanding of AI and its associated terms. Online platforms like Coursera and edX offer courses on AI and machine learning. Reading materials from reputable sources like Scribbr's Glossary of AI Terms and Wikipedia's comprehensive AI glossary can provide valuable insights.

This glossary is incomplete but is a starting point to demystify AI jargon. As the field of AI continues to evolve, so will the terminology. Staying current with these advances is crucial for anyone aiming to utilize AI effectively in their professional area.

1.4 THE EVOLUTION OF ARTIFICIAL INTELLIGENCE: FROM CONCEPT TO EVERYDAY APPLICATIONS

The history of artificial intelligence (AI) is an interesting journey through time. It is marked by important milestones that have brought us closer to creating machines with human-like intelligence. This chapter explores the rich history of AI, from its beginnings to the sophisticated systems we see today.

The Dawn of Artificial Neurons (1943)

In 1943, the seeds of AI were sown with the publication of a groundbreaking paper by Warren McCulloch and Walter Pitts. They introduced the concept of artificial neurons, proposing a computational model for neural networks. This idea laid the foundation for understanding how machines could simulate the workings of the human brain, sparking the imagination of scientists and researchers.

The Turing Machine (1950)

In 1950, the distinguished British mathematician Alan Turing introduced the Turing Test as a standard for evaluating machine intelligence. Turing's theoretical Turing Machine demonstrated that a simple device capable of reading and writing symbols on a tape could perform any conceivable mathematical computation if given the right algorithm and enough time. This concept became a cornerstone of computer science and AI, emphasizing the potential of machines to emulate human thought processes.

The Birth of Artificial Intelligence (1956)

The phrase "artificial intelligence" was first used in 1956 at the Dartmouth Conference, put together by John McCarthy, Nathaniel Rochester, Marvin Minsky, and Claude Shannon. This important event marked the official beginning of AI as a field of study. The conference brought together brilliant minds who shared a common vision: to create machines that could think, learn, and adapt.

The Perceptron and Early Neural Networks (1958)

In 1958, Frank Rosenblatt developed the perceptron, an early neural network model that mimicked the thought processes of the human brain. The perceptron paved the way for modern neural networks, making a big leap forward in the development of AI.

Lisp and Machine Learning (Late 1950s - Early 1960s)

Further progress was made in the late 1950s and early 1960s. John McCarthy invented Lisp, a programming language that became instrumental in AI research. Around the same time, Arthur Samuel introduced the concept of machine learning, teaching computers to improve their performance based on experience. These innovations were critical in shaping the future direction of AI research.

ELIZA and Natural Language Processing (1966)

Back in 1966, Joseph Weizenbaum came up with ELIZA, the very first chatbot. ELIZA mimicked conversation using pattern matching and substitution methodology, making it a basic but revolutionary advancement in natural language processing. This development showcased the potential of AI in understanding and generating human language.

The First AI Winter (1975-1980)

Despite the initial excitement, AI faced its first major setback in the mid-1970s. Known as the "AI Winter," this period was characterized by dwindling funding and interest due to unmet expectations and technical limitations. The hype surrounding AI had led to inflated promises, and when those promises went unfulfilled, skepticism grew. However, this phase also prompted researchers to reassess their approaches and set more realistic goals.

Intelligent Robots and Expert Systems (1970s - 1980s)

In 1970, Japan unveiled WABOT-1, the first intelligent humanoid robot capable of walking and interacting with its environment. During the same era, the development of expert systems—computer programs designed to mimic the decision-making abilities of a human expert—marked significant progress in AI. These innovations showcased the diverse applications of AI, from communication to robotics.

AI in the 1980s: A Second Writer and Renewed Hope

The late 1970s and early 1980s saw the emergence of AI in creative domains. AI systems like RACTER, a program developed in 1984, could generate random prose and poetry. Although not perfect, these early experiments demonstrated the potential for AI to engage in creative writing. This period also saw a resurgence of interest and funding, as advancements in computer hardware and software reignited optimism in the field.

Milestones in AI: Chess and Consumer Robots

In 1997, IBM's Deep Blue made history by defeating world chess champion Garry Kasparov. This victory was a landmark moment, proving that machines could outperform humans in complex strategic games. Five years later, in 2002, iRobot launched the Roomba, a vacuum cleaning robot that brought AI into everyday households. Roomba's ability to navigate and clean autonomously was a clear demonstration of AI's practical applications in consumer products.

Recent Breakthroughs: Dexterity, Assistants, and OpenAI

The 21st century has seen remarkable progress in AI. In 2019,

OpenAI's Dactyl trained itself to solve a Rubik's Cube with one hand, showcasing advanced dexterity and learning capabilities. A year earlier, in 2018, Google Duplex amazed the world with its ability to make phone calls and schedule appointments, blurring the lines between human and machine interactions.

Virtual assistants like Alexa, Siri, and Google Assistant have become ubiquitous, evolving from simple voice-activated tools to sophisticated AI companions. Silicon Valley becoming a tech hotspot has really sped up AI research and development. OpenAI, co-founded by Elon Musk and Sam Altman, is at the forefront of developing advanced, general-purpose AI.

Additional Historical Milestones

1. **1961**: Unimate, the first industrial robot, began working on a General Motors assembly line, showcasing the practical applications of robotics in manufacturing.
2. **1980**: The development of the XCON expert system by Digital Equipment Corporation demonstrated the commercial viability of AI in business applications.
3. **2011**: IBM's Watson defeated Jeopardy champions, highlighting AI's capabilities in natural language processing and information retrieval.
4. **2016**: AlphaGo, Google's AI program, managed to beat the world champion Go player Lee Sedol, showing how powerful deep learning and reinforcement learning can be.

Breakthrough Technologies

Key technological breakthroughs that propelled AI include deep learning, generative adversarial networks (GANs), and transformers. Deep learning techniques, popularized by researchers like John Hopfield and David Rumelhart, enabled computers to learn from experience, significantly enhancing their capabilities. GANs, introduced by Ian Goodfellow and colleagues, and transformers, developed by Google researchers, have revolutionized the ability of AI to generate realistic images, texts, and even deepfakes, showcasing the vast potential of AI in creative and analytical applications.

AI in Daily Life

Today, AI is seamlessly integrated into daily life, often in unnoticed ways, enhancing convenience, efficiency, and personalization. Smart assistants like Siri, Alexa, and Google Assistant use natural language processing to understand and respond to our queries, making interactions more intuitive. Recommendation systems on platforms like YouTube, Netflix, Spotify, and Amazon analyze our preferences to suggest movies, music, and products tailored to our tastes. AI-powered navigation apps, such as Google Maps and Waze, optimize routes and provide real-time traffic updates, saving us time and reducing stress. Additionally, AI drives the development of self-driving cars, revolutionizing transportation, and has led to significant advancements in healthcare, entertainment, and various other industries. These examples illustrate how AI seamlessly enhances our daily activities, often in ways we might not even realize.

How AI Is Changing the Business World

AI significantly streamlines business operations by automating repetitive tasks. In manufacturing, AI-powered robots handle assembly lines with precision and speed. In customer service, chatbots provide instant responses to common queries, improving customer satisfaction and freeing human agents for more complex issues. These applications enhance efficiency and reduce operational costs, allowing businesses to focus on innovation and growth.

Data Analysis and Decision Making

AI is crucial in analyzing large amounts of data to find patterns and insights in the age of big data. Machine learning algorithms sift through data to identify trends, predict outcomes, and inform strategic decisions. AI-driven analytics can help businesses understand customer behavior, optimize supply chains, and forecast market trends, leading to more informed and effective decision-making.

Personalization in Marketing

AI transforms marketing by enabling highly personalized customer experiences. By analyzing consumer data, AI can tailor marketing campaigns to individual preferences and behaviors. Personalized recommendations, targeted advertisements, and dynamic content adjustments based on user interactions increase engagement and conversion rates. This level of personalization significantly enhances customer satisfaction, drives sales, and fosters unwavering brand loyalty.

Future Prospects of AI

The journey of AI is a testament to human ingenuity and perseverance. From the theoretical musings of early pioneers to the tangible advancements of today, AI continues to evolve, transforming our world in unprecedented ways. As we look to the future, the potential for AI seems boundless, promising to reshape industries, enhance human capabilities, and perhaps even redefine what it means to be intelligent.

The future of AI holds promising advancements with the potential to revolutionize society and the economy further. Innovations in AI language processing, real-time translation, and autonomous vehicles are just the beginning. The long-term goal of achieving general intelligence, where machines surpass human cognitive abilities across all tasks, remains a fascinating yet ethically complex horizon. As artificial intelligence progresses, it will increasingly prompt important discussions on machine ethics and policies. This underscores the necessity for a strategic approach that maximizes AI's advantages while minimizing its potential hazards.

These insights underscore the dynamic nature of AI's evolution, from theoretical underpinnings to transformative technologies that redefine the possibilities of machine intelligence and its role in shaping the future.

1.5 HOW AI IS TRANSFORMING INDUSTRIES: A GLOBAL PERSPECTIVE

Industry Disruption

AI is revolutionizing industries by introducing innovative business models and opportunities. From transportation to agriculture, AI is enhancing efficiency and productivity by automating processes, optimizing logistics, and predicting outcomes. For example, in manufacturing, AI applications range from research and development to predictive analytics and real-time operations management. This shift is optimizing current processes and paving the way for new ways of conducting business across various sectors.

Global Adoption and Impact

The global impact of AI is profound, with predictions stating that AI could boost global GDP by 14% by 2030, translating to an additional $15.7 trillion to the global economy. This growth is attributed to AI's transformative potential across healthcare, agriculture, and public services industries. Developing economies are particularly optimistic about AI's benefits, expecting significant positive effects on growth, productivity, innovation, and job creation.

Success Stories

There are numerous success stories of businesses leveraging AI for growth. For instance, AI is being utilized in healthcare for risk management, analytics, and improving patient engagement. An exemplary illustration of this is Adaptive Technology's employment of Artificial Intelligence (AI) to interpret the immune system's signals to avert illnesses. In the retail sector, AI is improving customer service and predictive analytics, as seen with Lowe's introduction of LoweBots— autonomous robots that assist with inventory management powered by AI.

Challenges and Considerations

Despite the potential and successes of AI, there are significant challenges and considerations in its adoption. Ethical concerns, such as privacy and bias, are at the forefront, requiring careful consideration and regulation. The need for skilled labor to develop and manage AI technologies also poses a challenge, highlighting the importance of education and training in this evolving field. Moreover, there's a need for global and regional regulatory frameworks to ensure AI's ethical use and manage its societal impacts effectively.

In conclusion, AI is undeniably transforming industries globally, offering unprecedented opportunities for innovation and efficiency. However, a collaborative approach involving businesses, governments, and the workforce is crucial to harnessing its potential while fully mitigating risks.

1.6 THE ETHICS OF AI: BALANCING INNOVATION WITH RESPONSIBILITY

Ethical Principles in AI

The core ethical principles guiding the development and use of AI technologies are essential to ensure these advancements benefit humanity while minimizing potential harm. UNESCO identifies respect for human rights and dignity as foundational, emphasizing transparency, fairness, and human oversight of AI systems. The organization underscores the importance of embedding these principles across various policy areas, including data governance and environmental sustainability.

Addressing Bias and Fairness

Bias in AI algorithms poses a significant challenge, necessitating concerted efforts to ensure fairness in AI-driven decisions. UNESCO's ethics recommendation emphasizes the principle of fairness and non-discrimination, urging AI actors to promote social justice and ensure that the benefits of AI are accessible to all without exacerbating existing inequalities. This approach requires continuous assessment and adjustment of AI systems to mitigate biases and uphold equity.

Transparency and Accountability

Transparency and accountability are paramount for the ethical deployment of AI. These principles ensure that AI systems are auditable and traceable and that their impacts can be evaluated in alignment with human rights standards. UNESCO stresses the need for oversight, impact assessment, and due diligence to ensure that AI technologies do not conflict with human rights norms or threaten environmental well-being.

Future Ethical Considerations

As AI technology evolves, so will the ethical dilemmas and questions it raises. Adopting a dynamic understanding of AI is crucial, recognizing the rapid pace of technological change and the need for policies that can adapt over time. UNESCO's broad interpretation of AI as systems resembling intelligent behavior highlights the importance of future-proofing ethical guidelines against technological advancements.

The exploration and deployment of AI are entangled with ethical dilemmas that impact present-day use and have far-reaching future consequences. Ethical frameworks, such as UNESCO's global standard on AI ethics, provide a foundation for addressing these challenges. However, realizing these principles into actionable policies requires collaborative efforts among policymakers, technologists, and society to navigate the complexities of AI ethics and ensure responsible innovation.

For more detailed discussions on ethical principles in AI, you can explore the resources from UNESCO and insights shared by the World Economic Forum.

1.7 IDENTIFYING YOUR AI READINESS: SELF-ASSESSMENT FOR BEGINNERS

Embarking on an AI journey involves more than just enthusiasm for technology. It requires clearly understanding your objectives, assessing your technical skills, knowing the resources available, and a commitment to continuous learning. Below is a guide to help you self-assess your AI readiness.

Understanding Your Goals

Firstly, clarify what you aim to achieve with AI. Goals vary widely, from enhancing business operations through automation to generating passive income or improving customer experiences. Identifying your goals will direct your focus towards relevant AI applications and technologies. It's essential to ensure that your AI projects align with your business's strategic vision to avoid pursuing projects that, while interesting, don't contribute to your overarching objectives.

Assessing Technical Skills

Assessing your organization's current technical skills is crucial. This includes evaluating expertise in data science, machine learning, and IT infrastructure. While you might collaborate with AI solution providers, having in-house knowledge is beneficial for effective implementation and ongoing management of AI projects. Moreover, consider whether your team is equipped with or willing to acquire the necessary AI and data literacy skills.

Resource Availability

The success of AI projects heavily relies on the availability of high-quality data and the necessary computing infrastructure. Assess your organization's data management practices, including data collection, storage, and processing capabilities. Also, evaluate your organization's legal and technical aspects of data use. Having a robust data strategy is indispensable for successful AI implementation.

Commitment to Continuous Learning

The field of AI is rapidly evolving, with new advancements and tools emerging regularly. Maintaining a commitment to ongoing education is crucial for keeping up to date with the latest advancements, tools, and ethical issues in the realm of AI. This includes understanding the strategic and innovative aspects of AI, execution capabilities, and fostering a culture that values experimentation and adaptive learning.

By carefully considering these aspects, you can gauge your readiness to embark on AI projects and identify areas for further development. Remember, AI readiness is not solely about having the right tools or technologies but also about aligning your organizational strategy, culture, and resources toward effective and responsible AI adoption.

1.8 SETTING REALISTIC EXPECTATIONS: WHAT AI CAN AND CAN'T DO FOR YOU

Myth vs. Reality

The landscape of AI is often muddled with myths about its capabilities. While AI has made significant strides, separating fact from fiction is vital. For instance, AI's success in specific tasks, such as playing games or predicting patterns from data, may not directly translate to a universal problem-solving ability. Generalizable systems that can learn anything—a common expectation from AI—are still developing despite progress in areas like transfer learning.

Limitations of AI

AI's current limitations underscore the importance of setting realistic project expectations. For example, the necessity for massive training data sets for deep learning or the challenges in generalizing learning from one context to another highlight the need for specific and well-defined use cases. Moreover, the explainability problem, where understanding AI's decision-making process is complicated due to its complex model structures, remains a critical concern, particularly in sectors where transparency is essential.

Potential for Income Generation

The potential for AI to generate passive income is real but requires a nuanced understanding of where AI can add value. For instance, AI applications that automate document-based processes or provide predictive maintenance insights offer tangible benefits. However, the effectiveness of AI in these areas depends significantly on the quality of the data and the specificity of the task. Simplifying workflows or automating specific tasks can lead to cost savings and efficiency gains, indirectly contributing to income generation.

Long-Term Considerations

Investing in AI requires a long-term perspective, considering the rapid pace of development and the ethical implications of technology deployment.

The flexibility of AI applications, the critical nature of perpetual education to stay aligned with technological progress, and the establishment of ethical guidelines to navigate AI's evolution and application are of utmost significance. As AI technologies evolve, businesses must remain agile, continuously reassessing their strategies to leverage AI responsibly and effectively.

Understanding what AI can and cannot do is crucial for businesses and individuals investing in this technology. By debunking common myths, acknowledging AI's limitations, and exploring its potential critically, stakeholders can set realistic expectations and plan for a future where AI contributes value responsibly and sustainably.

The field of Artificial Intelligence (AI) is constantly changing and advancing.

Common AI Myths

- **Myth 1**: AI can perform any intellectual task that a human can.
- **Myth 2**: AI can learn and understand emotions like humans.
- **Myth 3**: AI is on the verge of becoming sentient.

Debunking: AI's capabilities are impressive but are currently limited to tasks for which they are specifically designed and trained. Emotional understanding and sentience are beyond AI's current reach.

The Truth About AI and Jobs

- **Concern**: AI will replace all human jobs, leading to mass unemployment.
- **Reality**: While AI automates specific tasks, it also creates new job categories and enhances human productivity, leading to a shift in the job market rather than outright replacement.

AI Will Replace All Jobs

One of the most common misconceptions about AI is that it will lead to mass unemployment by replacing all jobs. While it's true that AI can automate repetitive tasks, it also creates new job categories and opportunities. AI enhances human capabilities rather than rendering them obsolete. For example, in healthcare, AI assists doctors by analyzing medical images, allowing them to focus on patient care and complex decision-making. AI chatbots handle routine inquiries in customer service, freeing human agents to tackle more nuanced and challenging problems. By automating specific tasks, AI enables humans to engage in more meaningful and creative work.

AI Can Surpass Human Intelligence Imminently

Another common misconception is that AI will soon surpass human intelligence and take over decision-making processes. However, the reality is far more nuanced. AI has made great progress in certain areas, but we're still working towards achieving true general intelligence. The objective is to develop AI systems that can comprehend, learn, and apply knowledge across a diverse range of tasks. Current AI systems excel in narrow tasks but lack the comprehensive cognitive abilities of humans. The development of general AI involves complex challenges that researchers are still working to overcome. Thus, the imminent arrival of superintelligent AI is more fiction than fact.

AI Is Inherently Biased

The belief that AI is inherently biased stems from instances where AI systems have exhibited biased behavior. It's important to understand that AI itself isn't inherently biased. Biases in AI systems come from the training data and developer decisions, rather than inherent flaws. If the training data contains biases, the AI model will likely reflect those biases. Efforts to create fair and transparent AI models are ongoing, with researchers and developers working on techniques to detect and mitigate biases. This is to ensure that AI systems are as unbiased and equitable as possible. The goal is to build AI that performs well and aligns with ethical standards and social fairness.

AI Is Only for Big Corporations

Many people believe that AI is a tool reserved for large corporations with vast resources. In reality, AI is increasingly accessible to small businesses and individual entrepreneurs. The proliferation of user-friendly AI platforms and services means that even those with limited technical expertise can leverage AI. Tools for automating marketing, analyzing customer data, and personalizing customer experiences are available at affordable prices. Additionally, many AI solutions are scalable, allowing businesses of all sizes to integrate AI into their operations. This democratization of AI technology means that anyone can harness its power to enhance their business and drive growth.

By debunking these myths, we can foster a more accurate understanding of AI and its potential. The following chapters will delve into practical strategies for leveraging AI to achieve financial freedom, providing you with the tools and knowledge to navigate the AI landscape effectively.

AI and Human Intelligence

- **Difference**: AI operates based on algorithms and data, needing a more nuanced understanding and adaptability of human intelligence.
- **Complementarity**: AI and human intelligence can complement each other, with AI handling data-driven tasks efficiently, freeing humans for creative and strategic roles.

Setting the Record Straight

- **Benefits**: From healthcare to education, AI has the potential to improve efficiency and outcomes significantly.
- **Limitations**: AI systems can be biased, require vast data, and cannot replicate human creativity or ethical reasoning.

In this context, understanding the limitations and realistic capabilities of AI is crucial. AI tools, ranging from language models like GPT-4 to specialized applications in healthcare diagnostics, underscore the technology's vast potential and its dependence on human oversight for ethical and creative decision-making.

1.9 THE ROLE OF AI IN CREATING PASSIVE INCOME

Automated Revenue Streams

One of the most compelling aspects of AI is its ability to automate tasks, leading to the creation of passive income streams that require minimal ongoing effort. AI-driven automation can handle repetitive and time-consuming tasks such as email marketing, customer service interactions, and even product recommendations in online stores. For instance, AI chatbots can manage customer inquiries 24/7, while automated email campaigns can nurture leads and drive sales without constant human intervention. These automated systems work tirelessly, generating revenue around the clock and freeing up your time to focus on strategic growth or other ventures.

Enhanced Investment Strategies

AI's impact on financial markets has been profound, particularly in the realm of investment strategies. Algorithmic trading, with the help of AI, uses smart algorithms to make trades at the best times based on specific criteria, often doing so faster and more accurately than human traders. Predictive analytics, another AI application, analyzes vast amounts of financial data to forecast market trends and inform investment decisions. These technologies enable investors to make data-driven decisions, potentially increasing returns while mitigating risks. By leveraging AI in investment strategies, you can create a more robust and automated approach to growing your wealth.

Content Creation and Curation

AI-driven platforms are revolutionizing content creation and curation, making it possible to generate scalable content with minimal effort. Tools like AI writers can produce blog posts, social media updates, and even video scripts, tailored to specific audiences and optimized for engagement. For example, AI can analyze trending topics and generate relevant content ideas, or it can automate the editing and publishing process for videos. These platforms allow content creators to maintain a consistent online presence and attract a steady stream of visitors, which can be monetized through advertising, sponsorships, or affiliate marketing.

E-commerce Optimization

E-commerce businesses can significantly benefit from AI tools that optimize various aspects of online store performance. AI-driven inventory management systems ensure that stock levels are maintained efficiently, reducing the risk of overstocking or stockouts. Personalization engines analyze customer behavior and preferences to deliver tailored shopping experiences, increasing customer satisfaction and conversion rates. Additionally, AI can optimize pricing strategies and recommend products, enhancing sales and profitability. By integrating these AI tools, e-commerce entrepreneurs can create a more efficient, profitable, and passive income-generating business model.

As we continue to explore the transformative power of AI, it becomes evident that these technologies offer vast potential for creating passive income. The next chapters will provide detailed guides and practical strategies for leveraging AI in various aspects of your financial journey, equipping you with the tools to achieve financial freedom and independence.

1.10 Identifying AI Opportunities in Your Life

Skillset and Interest Alignment

The first step in leveraging AI to create opportunities in your life is to evaluate your existing skills and interests. Identifying areas where your strengths align with AI applications can help you choose the most suitable and enjoyable paths. For instance, if you have a background in data analysis, you might find opportunities in AI-driven data analytics or machine learning. If you have a passion for content creation, exploring AI tools for automated writing or video production could be rewarding. Reflect on your hobbies, professional experiences, and the tasks you enjoy, then research AI tools that can enhance or automate those activities.

Market Demand Assessment

Understanding market needs and identifying gaps that AI can fill is crucial for aligning AI opportunities with your financial goals. Start by researching industries that are rapidly adopting AI, such as healthcare, finance, retail, and marketing. Look for pain points within these sectors that AI can address, such as improving customer service, enhancing product recommendations, or streamlining operational processes. By focusing on high-demand areas, you can position yourself to capitalize on opportunities where AI solutions are most needed. Tools like market analysis reports, industry news, and trend forecasts can provide valuable insights into these opportunities.

Leveraging Existing Networks

Your existing networks and resources can be instrumental in finding AI opportunities in familiar domains. Reach out to colleagues, mentors, and professional associations to learn about AI applications in your field. Attend industry conferences, webinars, and workshops to connect with AI professionals and gain insights into emerging trends. By leveraging your network, you can discover practical AI applications and potential collaborations that align with your expertise. Additionally, online platforms like LinkedIn and specialized AI communities can be valuable resources for networking and staying updated on industry developments.

Continuous Learning and Adaptation

The field of AI is continually evolving, making continuous learning and adaptation essential. Stay updated on AI advancements by following reputable sources like academic journals, industry publications, and professional organizations. Consider online courses, workshops, or certifications to deepen your skills. Being adaptable and open to learning new methods will keep you ahead of the curve as AI technologies evolve. Regularly reassess your strategies and be open to experimenting with new AI tools and approaches to optimize your opportunities and outcomes.

By aligning your skills and interests with market demand, leveraging your networks, and committing to continuous learning, you can effectively identify and capitalize on AI opportunities in your life. The following chapters will delve deeper into practical applications and strategies, providing you with the knowledge and tools to harness AI for financial growth and personal fulfillment.

AI is reshaping the workforce, creating new opportunities while rendering some traditional roles obsolete. Routine tasks are increasingly being automated, necessitating a shift in skill sets. Jobs that require creativity, critical thinking, and emotional intelligence are becoming more valuable. AI also opens up new career paths in AI development, data science, and AI ethics. Embracing continuous learning and adaptability is essential for staying relevant in the evolving job market.

By understanding the basics of AI and its profound impact on various aspects of life and business, you are well-equipped to explore how AI can transform your financial future. In the next chapters, we'll explore using AI for financial freedom.

CHAPTER 2
CHATGPT

2.1 A BRIEF HISTORY OF CHATGPT

ChatGPT, developed by OpenAI, has rapidly evolved since its introduction in November 2022. This conversational AI model is based on the Generative Pre-trained Transformer (GPT) architecture, which uses deep learning to produce human-like text responses.

Key Milestones in ChatGPT's Development:

1. **GPT-1 to GPT-3**: The journey began with the release of GPT-1 in 2018, featuring 117 million parameters. GPT-2 followed in 2019, with 1.5 billion parameters. GPT-3, launched in 2020, marked a significant leap with 175 billion parameters, setting a new standard for natural language processing models.

2. **InstructGPT**: In January 2022, OpenAI introduced InstructGPT, a fine-tuned version of GPT-3 designed to follow instructions more effectively and reduce the generation of harmful content.

3. **ChatGPT**: Launched in November 2022, ChatGPT quickly gained popularity due to its conversational abilities and user-friendly interface. Within five days, it had over 1 million users, and by January 2023, it reached 100 million

users, becoming one of the fastest-growing consumer applications in history.

4. **ChatGPT Plus and GPT-4**: In February 2023, OpenAI introduced ChatGPT Plus, a subscription service offering enhanced features. In March 2023, GPT-4 was released, bringing improved accuracy, creativity, and handling of complex tasks. GPT-4 also introduced multimodal capabilities, allowing it to process both text and images.

5. **Plugins and Integrations**: Throughout 2023, OpenAI expanded ChatGPT's functionality by introducing plugins and integrations. These included web browsing, code interpretation, and interactions with third-party services, significantly enhancing the model's versatility and practical applications.

6. **GPT-4o**: In 2024, OpenAI released GPT-4o, an optimized version of GPT-4, offering improved performance across text, voice, and vision tasks. This model further refined the capabilities of GPT-4, making it more efficient and versatile for a wide range of applications.

User Growth and Impact:

By 2024, ChatGPT has become a global phenomenon with millions of users. It is used in various sectors, including education, customer service, content creation, and more. The continuous improvements and the introduction of new features have solidified its place as a leading AI tool in the market.

2.2 HOW TO USE CHATGPT: TRANSFORMING BUSINESS AND CONTENT CREATION

In today's fast-paced world, leveraging advanced technologies like ChatGPT can significantly benefit entrepreneurs and content creators. This chapter will guide you through the essential concepts and practical applications for using ChatGPT effectively, with a focus on making money online. By mastering these techniques, you can streamline operations, enhance customer experiences, and innovate your content strategies.

Understanding ChatGPT

ChatGPT, developed by OpenAI, is a versatile language model designed to generate human-like text based on given prompts. It excels in tasks such as content creation, customer support, and market research. Understanding how to craft effective prompts and use system messages to guide its responses is key to maximizing its potential.

Key Features

ChatGPT's capabilities include:

- **Impressive Natural Language Understanding and Generation**: It can comprehend and generate human-like text.
- **Handling a Wide Range of Prompts and Questions**: Capable of addressing various topics and queries.
- **Content Generation**: Writing articles, blogs, and social media posts.
- **Customer Support**: Automate responding to common customer inquiries to free up your support team to handle more complex issues.
- **Market Research**: Analyze trends and competitors, providing valuable insights to inform business strategies.
- **Sales and Marketing**: Craft persuasive pitches and marketing content to boost business growth.
- **Virtual Assistants**: Providing information, answering questions, and performing tasks.

Limitations

Despite its capabilities, ChatGPT has some limitations:

- **Factually Incorrect but Plausible-Sounding Responses**: ChatGPT may generate responses that seem correct but are factually wrong.
- **Sensitive to Input Phrasing**: The way a question is phrased can significantly affect the response.

Potential Use Cases

ChatGPT can be utilized in various applications, including:

- **Content Generation**: Creating articles, blog posts, and creative writing.
- **Language Translation**: Translating text between languages.
- **Virtual Assistants**: Providing information, answering questions, and performing tasks.
- **Improved Productivity**: Handling routine queries and tasks to free up human resources for more complex activities.

Benefits

Using ChatGPT offers several benefits:

- **Personalized Interactions**: Understands context for engaging user experiences.
- **Accessibility**: Provides support anytime and anywhere.
- **Language Adaptability**: Communicates in multiple languages for global markets.

Crafting Effective Prompts

To obtain accurate and relevant responses, it's crucial to formulate clear and specific questions. Here are some steps and examples to help you get started:

Formulating Clear Questions

Clear and specific questions help ChatGPT understand your intent better.

Example:

- Instead of: "Tell me about marketing."
- Use: "What are the top three digital marketing strategies for coaches in 2024?"

Providing Context and Constraints

Provide context to make responses more relevant. Include constraints like response length or tone.

Example:

- Prompt: "Write a 200-word introduction to a blog post about digital art, aimed at young professionals."
- Output: ChatGPT will generate a concise, targeted introduction that fits the specified context and length.

Handling Ambiguity

Ambiguity can lead to irrelevant responses. Refine prompts iteratively until clarity is achieved.

Example:

- Initial Prompt: "Tell me about social media."
- Refined Prompt: "Explain how X can be used for influencer marketing, focusing on engagement strategies."

Leveraging System Messages

System messages significantly influence ChatGPT's behavior. These messages set the tone, provide context, or steer the conversation flow.

Examples of System Messages

- **Setting the Tone**: "You are a business consultant. Provide advice in a professional and concise manner."
- **Guiding Responses**: "Answer the following questions with a focus on practical applications for small businesses."

2.3 PRACTICAL APPLICATIONS FOR ENTREPRENEURS AND CONTENT CREATORS

Streamlining Business Processes

Automate tasks like generating invoices, drafting emails, and creating project plans.

Example:

- Prompt: "Outline a detailed project plan for launching a digital product within two months."

- Output: ChatGPT will generate a step-by-step project plan, including key milestones and resources needed.

Enhancing Customer Experience

Personalize interactions by generating follow-up emails, addressing FAQs, and crafting social media content.

Example:

- Prompt: "Write a personalized follow-up email to a customer who recently purchased a mobile phone."
- Output: ChatGPT will create a customized email thanking the customer and offering additional resources or support.

Conducting Market Research

Summarize industry reports, analyze competitor strategies, and identify emerging trends.

Example:

- Prompt: "Summarize the key findings from the latest industry report on the sustainable fashion market."
- Output: ChatGPT will provide a concise summary, highlighting the main insights and trends.

Managing Model Behavior and Bias

It's essential to recognize and address biases in language models. Regularly review and refine the model's behavior using clear, explicit instructions to guide its responses. Implementing pre- and post-processing steps helps filter or modify outputs to mitigate harmful or untruthful responses.

Enhancing Responses with User Instructions

Specify the desired response format to improve the structure and organization of the outputs. Request clarification or elaboration to prompt specific and detailed responses. Provide explicit guidance by breaking down complex questions and offering examples.

Example:

- Prompt: "Explain the importance of SEO for small businesses, using bullet points."
- Output: ChatGPT will generate a structured list of SEO benefits for small businesses.

Iterative Feedback and Fine-Tuning

Collecting feedback is crucial for improving ChatGPT's performance. Use reinforcement learning techniques to optimize responses based on user feedback. Fine-tune models for specific tasks or domains to enhance their performance and relevance.

Example:

- Prompt: "Create a customer satisfaction survey for an online bookstore."
- Output: ChatGPT will draft a survey with questions targeting key areas of customer satisfaction.

Best Practices and Future Developments

Ensure responses are accurate, unbiased, and respectful. Stay updated with advancements such as multimodal capabilities and personalized interactions. OpenAI is working on methods for greater user control over ChatGPT's behavior.

Setting Up and Accessing ChatGPT

Understand how to obtain and manage API keys securely. Utilize software development kits (SDKs) and libraries in various programming languages to integrate ChatGPT into applications.

Example:

- Use the OpenAI Python library to send a prompt to ChatGPT and receive a response:

```
import openai openai.api_key = 'YOUR_API_KEY' response = openai.Completion.create(engine="text-davinci-003", prompt="What is the weather in London today?", max_tokens=50) print(response.choices[0].text.strip())
```

• • •

Instructions for Using ChatGPT to Find Online Business Ideas

1. **Open ChatGPT:**
2. Navigate to the ChatGPT platform.
3. **Copy and Paste the Prompts:**
4. Select one of the prompts listed below.
5. Copy the selected prompt (highlight the text, right-click, and select 'Copy' or press **Ctrl+C** on Windows/**Command+C** on Mac).
6. **Enter the Prompt in ChatGPT:**
7. Click on the input box in ChatGPT.
8. Paste the copied prompt into the input box (right-click and select 'Paste' or press **Ctrl+V** on Windows/**Command+V** on Mac).
9. Press 'Enter' to submit the prompt.
10. **Review the Response:**
11. Read the response generated by ChatGPT. It will provide suggestions and ideas based on the prompt.
12. **Repeat for Each Prompt:**
13. Follow steps 2 to 4 for each of the following prompts to gather a comprehensive list of online business ideas and strategies.

Prompts

1. What are some online business ideas that are suitable for someone just starting out?
2. I'm interested in launching an online business with minimal upfront costs. What do you recommend?
3. Can you provide some examples of online businesses that can make a positive social impact?
4. What are some online business ideas that have the potential for rapid growth?
5. I'd like to start an online business in the tech industry. Any tips on where to begin?

6. What are some easy-to-manage online businesses for beginners?

7. Can you suggest online business ideas that can be started with little technical knowledge?

8. I want to start an online business in the health and wellness industry. Do you have any recommendations on how to get started?

9. What are some profitable online business ideas that don't require extensive experience?

10. Can you recommend some online business ideas that are both beginner-friendly and scalable?

Additional Tips

- **Save Useful Responses:**
- If you find any particularly helpful responses, consider saving them for future reference.
- **Ask Follow-Up Questions:**
- Feel free to ask further questions or for clarification on any of the ideas provided by ChatGPT.
- **Explore Different Angles:**
- Experiment with modifying the prompts slightly to explore different angles or more specific aspects of online business ideas.

All prompts are available for download at: https://aiwealthentrepreneur.com/tools

Using Polite Phrases

Using polite phrases like "please" and "thank you" in ChatGPT prompts doesn't significantly alter the substance of the responses. However, there are nuances worth noting:

1. **Politeness and Response Quality**: Some users report that including polite phrases can lead to slightly longer or more detailed responses. For instance, an informal test found that prompts with offers of tips (e.g., "I'll give you a tip if you help") resulted in more detailed responses. This suggests that the model might subtly adjust its output based on perceived user politeness, although this isn't a consistent or scientifically validated outcome.
2. **Human-like Interaction**: Including polite phrases like "please" and "thank you" can make the interaction feel more natural and human-like. This can be beneficial for maintaining a positive user experience, even though the AI itself doesn't require politeness to function effectively.
3. **Contextual Adjustments**: In some cases, adding politeness might change the tone of the response. For example, "Can you help me with this, please?" might yield a slightly more engaging or friendly response compared to "Help me with this." However, the core information provided by the AI remains largely unchanged.

In summary, while politeness in prompts doesn't fundamentally change the output's quality or accuracy, it can influence the tone and length of responses, contributing to a more positive interaction. It's more about enhancing the user experience than improving the AI's performance. By mastering ChatGPT and integrating it with other AI tools, entrepreneurs and content creators can streamline operations, enhance customer experiences, and make informed decisions. Staying updated with advancements in AI will ensure continuous leverage of these technologies for growth.

2.4 TOP CHATGPT CHROME EXTENSIONS FOR BEGINNERS

For those just starting out with enhancing their ChatGPT experience on Chrome, there are several easy-to-use extensions that can make your interactions more robust and streamlined. Here's a beginner-friendly overview of some top picks:

1. **For Uploading Files to ChatGPT**: There's an extension ("ChatGPT File Uploader Extended") that lets you easily upload various file types, such as PDFs and Word documents, directly to ChatGPT. This is especially handy if you're using the accessible version of ChatGPT and still want the benefits of file uploads.
2. **Writing Assistant**: Imagine having a helper for writing emails and messages in your browser. There's an extension designed for this ("ChatGPT Writer", "QuillBot"), simplifying the way you compose text on all websites. It's straightforward to use: log in and start typing.
3. **Reading Aid**: If you often find web content hard to digest, look for an extension that simplifies complex information, such as "Wiseone." It works by automatically breaking down challenging text into easier-to-understand pieces.
4. **Browser-Wide Assistance**: Want ChatGPT's help across your entire browser, not just on specific sites? An extension such as "Merlin" makes ChatGPT accessible on any webpage with a simple shortcut. It's like having a ChatGPT companion wherever you go online.
5. **Integrating Web Results**: Some extensions can bring real-time web information into your ChatGPT conversations, such as "WebChatGPT," making the responses more accurate and up-to-date. This is great for research or when you need the latest info.
6. **Voice Commands**: For those who prefer speaking to typing, some extensions, such as "Prometheus," allow you to talk to ChatGPT. Just hold down a button and tell your query. It's a quick way to communicate without needing to type everything out.

These tools are great for beginners looking to maximize ChatGPT in their Chrome browser. They can help with everything from managing workloads to simplifying complex reading material while enhancing your browsing experience.

2.5 COMPARING LEADING AI MODELS: OPENAI CHATGPT, MICROSOFT COPILOT, GOOGLE GEMINI, AND ANTHROPIC CLAUDE 3

OpenAI's ChatGPT, Microsoft Copilot, Google Gemini, and Anthropic Claude 3 represent the forefront of AI-driven productivity tools, each with unique strengths and potential drawbacks.

OpenAI ChatGPT:

- **Costs**: ChatGPT offers a free tier with access to GPT-3.5 and a paid subscription, ChatGPT Plus, at $20 plus VAT per month for access to GPT-4, and GPT-40.
- **Token Limits**: GPT-3.5 has a context window of approximately 4,000 tokens, while GPT-4 can handle up to 8,000 tokens or 32,000 tokens in its extended version.
- **Advantages**: Known for its conversational prowess and versatility, it excels in generating human-like text across various applications. Extensive plugin support enhances its functionality.
- **Disadvantages**: Requires careful prompt engineering to avoid biases and inaccuracies.

Microsoft Copilot:

- **Costs**: Included with Microsoft 365 subscriptions, which range from $6.99 to $22 per month per user.
- **Token Limits**: Not explicitly mentioned as it integrates within Microsoft 365 applications, leveraging the underlying AI services' token limits.
- **Advantages**: this solution seamlessly integrates with Office 365 to make your work easier. It automates tasks and offers helpful suggestions in Word and Excel.
- **Disadvantages**: Functionality is tightly bound to the Microsoft ecosystem, potentially limiting its utility outside of this environment.

Google Gemini:

- **Costs**: Pricing details are not publicly disclosed and may vary based on usage and integration needs.
- **Token Limits**: Specific token limits are not detailed, but Google's AI services typically handle large context windows effectively.
- **Advantages**: Stands out with multimodal capabilities, processing both text and images to deliver rich, context-aware responses. Highly versatile for diverse applications, from creative projects to data analysis.
- **Disadvantages**: Privacy concerns and data usage policies may be a drawback for some users.

Anthropic Claude 3:

- **Costs**: Anthropic's pricing is generally enterprise-focused and customized based on specific needs and usage volumes.
- **Token Limits**: Claude 3 supports a context window of up to 100,000 tokens, allowing for extensive and detailed interactions.
- **Advantages**: Developed with a focus on ethical AI, prioritizing safe and reliable outputs. Aims to minimize harmful content and provide transparent responses.
- **Disadvantages**: May lag behind in terms of raw performance and the breadth of features compared to its competitors.

Understanding Tokens: Tokens are pieces of words used by AI models to process and generate text. For example, "ChatGPT is great!" would be split into six tokens:

["Chat", "GPT", " is", " great", "!"]. Token limits refer to the maximum number of tokens a model can process in a single interaction. Higher token limits allow for more extensive conversations and complex queries, enhancing the AI's ability to understand and generate relevant responses.

Prompt Chaining and Negative Prompts: Prompt chaining involves linking multiple prompts together to guide the AI through a sequence of tasks, improving the depth and accuracy of responses.

Negative prompts are used to specify what the AI should avoid, ensuring outputs are more aligned with user expectations by preventing undesirable content.

Each of these AI tools offers distinct advantages tailored to specific needs, whether it's ChatGPT's broad adaptability, Copilot's productivity enhancements, Gemini's multimodal prowess, or Claude 3's ethical considerations.

Understanding these differences, costs, and token limits will help you to choose the right tool for your specific requirements.

CHAPTER 3

CREATING MULTIPLE PASSIVE INCOME STREAMS WITH AI

3.1 THE BASICS OF PASSIVE INCOME WITH AI: AN OVERVIEW

Understanding Passive Income

Passive income, in the AI context, refers to earnings derived from digital platforms and tools that, once set up, require minimal ongoing effort. AI's automation capabilities play a pivotal role in sustaining these income streams by handling repetitive tasks, data analysis, and operational management efficiently.

AI's Role in Passive Income Generation

AI technologies automate complex tasks and analyze vast datasets to identify opportunities, trends, and insights. This automation is crucial in areas like content creation, where AI can generate articles, blog posts, or even videos, significantly reducing the manual workload and facilitating a steady income flow with less effort.

Types of AI-Enabled Passive Income Streams

Several passive income streams are particularly well-suited to AI integration:

- **Affiliate Marketing**: Using AI to optimize affiliate marketing strategies, from personalized product recommendations to targeted content creation.

- **Digital Product Sales**: Using AI tools to develop and promote digital products, such as eBooks, courses, or software.
- **Online Courses**: Employing AI to curate and personalize learning experiences, making online education more accessible and scalable.

Setting Realistic Expectations

While AI opens up new avenues for generating passive income, it's crucial to approach these opportunities with realistic expectations. Success in AI-driven passive income requires understanding the technology, the market, and the time investment needed to create and maintain these income streams effectively.

For more detailed insights and practical examples of creating passive income streams with AI, resources such as Forbes (https://www.forbes.com) and TechCrunch (https://techcrunch.com) regularly publish articles on the latest trends and success stories in the AI space. Additionally, online learning platforms like Coursera (https://www.coursera.org) offer courses that can help you understand and leverage AI for your passive income projects.

It is exciting to embark on the journey of creating passive income streams with AI. By understanding the basics, exploring the types of income streams available, setting realistic goals, and continuously learning, you can leverage AI to achieve financial success with minimal ongoing effort.

The article on Wix's blog outlines innovative ways to use AI for income generation, such as building websites, creating AI-generated artwork, becoming a YouTube content creator, producing online courses, entering affiliate marketing, and starting a resume business. Each method utilizes AI's capabilities to streamline processes and enhance productivity in various domains.

Creating passive income using AI tools offers a wide range of possibilities for beginners looking to leverage technology to generate revenue with minimal ongoing effort. Here's a summary of various strategies and tools you can use to start your journey toward earning passive income through AI:

- **Chatbots and Virtual Assistants**: Develop and deploy AI-powered chatbots for businesses to automate customer service and support tasks, creating an opportunity for passive income through service sales.
- **Predictive Modeling**: AI can be employed to construct anticipatory models for financial forecasts, analysis of customer behavior, and other similar applications. These models can be marketed and sold to investors, financial institutions, and companies.
- **Content Creation**: AI can create unique content such as articles, blogs, and posts to boost web traffic and increase earnings through ads and affiliate marketing.
- **E-commerce Optimization**: AI tools can enhance e-commerce experiences by personalizing shopping experiences, managing inventory, and automating customer service, contributing to increased sales and passive income.
- **Trading**: Leveraging AI and machine learning algorithms for trading and investments can potentially generate passive income, though it requires knowledge and understanding of the field.
- **YouTube Automation**: Creating a niche YouTube channel and using AI for tasks like research, optimization, scriptwriting, and video editing can generate passive income through advertising revenue, sponsorships, and more.
- **AI Investment Advisory**: Utilize AI models for data analysis and predictive analytics to manage investment portfolios, offering services to clients or for personal investments.
- **Investing in AI Companies**: Direct investment in companies' stocks leading the AI technology wave can yield passive income through dividends and capital gains.
- **Digital Products**: Enhance digital products like e-books, online courses, and webinars with AI for personalization, increasing their value and appeal.
- **AI-Based Consultation Services**: Offer consultation services powered by AI's data analysis for financial planning, career coaching, and more.

- **Mobile Apps and Games**: Develop AI-powered apps or games that provide tailored user experiences, monetized through in-app purchases or ads.

Additionally, innovative strategies for using AI to generate passive income include:

- **Technical Troubleshooting Guides**: Create guides for solving software or hardware issues, marketing them to companies or directly to consumers.
- **Automated Social Media Engagement Plans**: Develop automated posts and engagement strategies for businesses to maintain an active online presence. These plans can be sold on a subscription basis.
- **Interactive Story Apps**: Write and monetize complex, branching storylines in app form, offering a "choose-your-own-adventure" experience.
- **Literary Analysis and Study Guides**: Generate in-depth analyses or guides for classic literature, potentially serving educational institutions or literature enthusiasts.
- **Meditation and Mindfulness Scripts**: Utilize AI to write scripts for guided meditations, which can be voiced and sold as tracks or apps.
- **Legal Document Templates**: Produce templates for standard legal documents, offering them as digital products for download.

For more details on leveraging AI tools to generate passive income and various strategies for beginners, please refer to the following resources:

- **Plain English**: Provides insights into using AI for different passive income streams. Accessed at: https://www.plainenglish.io.

- **Ippei Blog**: Offers strategies for generating passive income through AI, including content creation and automation. Accessed at: https://ippei.com.
- **Elegant Themes**: Discusses AI tools that can be utilized to enhance digital marketing efforts and generate passive income. Accessed at: https://www.elegantthemes.com.
- **GOBankingRates**: Highlights ways AI can be applied to create passive income opportunities, including investments in AI companies. Accessed at: https://www.gobankingrates.com.
- **Geeky Gadgets**: Lists 25+ AI passive income ideas and strategies, from automated social media plans to creating digital products like e-books. Accessed at: https://www.geeky-gadgets.com.

These references offer valuable perspectives and actionable strategies for utilizing AI tools to create passive income streams, catering to various interests and skill levels.

1. **AI-Powered Blogging**: Use AI to generate unique blog content on niche topics. Monetize through ads, affiliate marketing, or sponsored content.
2. **AI-Enhanced Stock Trading**: Employ AI algorithms for stock market analysis and predictions. Earn income through informed trading decisions.
3. **Virtual Event Planning with AI**: Leverage AI tools for organizing and managing virtual events. Charge for event planning services or through ticket sales.
4. **AI-Driven Freelance Services**: Offer AI-powered services such as data analysis, marketing strategy optimization, or customer insights reports to clients.
5. **AI Tutoring and Education Platforms**: Create an online education platform using AI to personalize learning experiences. Income can be generated through course fees.
6. **AI Personal Fitness Coaching**: Develop a fitness app that uses AI to tailor workout and nutrition plans. Monetize through subscription models.

7. **Custom AI Art Creation**: Use AI art generators to create custom artwork. You can sell the artwork online or offer commissioned pieces.

8. **AI Voiceover Services**: Utilize AI to generate voiceovers for videos, podcasts, or advertisements. Offer your services to content creators and marketers.

9. **AI-Powered Language Translation Services**: Offer translation services by leveraging AI translation tools, catering to businesses looking to globalize their content.

10. **Automated E-commerce Store Management**: Use AI tools for managing inventory, customer service, and personalized marketing in an e-commerce store. Revenue can come from sales and affiliate marketing.

These ideas highlight the versatility of AI tools in creating diverse income streams from the comfort of your home. By capitalizing on AI's ability to automate tasks, analyze data, and personalize experiences, you can explore various avenues for passive and active income online.

1. **AI-Assisted Movie Creation**: Utilize AI tools like **Runway ML** for video editing and effects, making it easier to produce high-quality movies from home. Monetize through platforms like YouTube or Vimeo on Demand.

2. **Content Writing with AI**: Employ AI writing assistants like **Jasper (formerly Jarvis)** to generate articles, blog posts, or e-books. Income can be derived from content sales, affiliate marketing, or freelance writing services.

3. **Social Media Marketing Automation**: Use AI tools such as **Buffer** or **Hootsuite**, integrated with AI for optimizing post times and content, to manage social media campaigns more efficiently. You can offer your assistance to companies seeking to improve their online visibility.

4. **AI-Generated Text for Copywriting**: **Copy.ai** can help create compelling marketing copy, emails, and product descriptions. Freelance copywriters can leverage this tool to increase productivity and take on more clients.

5. **Custom AI Art and Illustration**: **DeepArt** and **Sora** can transform photos into artwork in various styles. Sell artwork online or offer personalized art creation services.

6. **Video Editing with AI**: **CapCut** and **Adobe Premiere Pro** (with AI features) streamline video editing tasks, making it more straightforward to create professional-looking videos. Freelancers can offer video editing services or create their own content channels.

7. **AI-Powered Music Composition**: Tools like **AIVA** enable the creation of original music compositions using AI. You can compose music for films and video games or sell your tracks directly online.

8. **Automated Affiliate Marketing**: Use AI to analyze and select the best affiliate programs and optimize marketing strategies. Tools like **Affise** can help manage and automate your affiliate marketing efforts.

9. **AI for E-Book Writing and Publishing**: AI writing tools like **Sudowrite** can assist in generating creative fiction or non-fiction content. Self-publish through platforms like Amazon Kindle Direct Publishing for passive income.

10. **Voiceover and Podcast Production**: Leverage AI voice generation tools like **Descript's Overdub** for creating voiceovers for videos or producing podcast episodes. Monetize through podcast sponsorships or services offered to video creators.

These ideas showcase the versatility of AI in supporting creative and commercial endeavors online. By leveraging these tools, individuals can enhance their productivity, unleash their creativity, and open up new avenues for income generation from the comfort of their homes.

Leveraging Large Language Models (LLMs) for creative and commercial projects offers expansive possibilities across text, images, voice, and movie generation. Here are more innovative ideas, each paired with tools that harness the power of LLMs for content creation:

1. **Interactive Chatbots for Customer Service**: Create AI-driven chatbots using **OpenAI's GPT-3** to provide instant customer support on websites or social media platforms.

2. **Personalized Content Creation**: Use **Jasper AI** to generate customized blog posts, articles, or product descriptions tailored to specific audiences or SEO requirements.

3. **AI-Generated Art for Merchandise**: Leverage **DALL-E** by OpenAI for creating unique artwork or designs that can be printed on merchandise like t-shirts, mugs, or posters, sold through platforms such as Etsy or Redbubble.

4. **Voice Synthesis for Podcasts and Audiobooks**: Utilize **Descript's Overdub** to generate realistic voiceovers for podcasts, audiobooks, or video narration, allowing for content creation in multiple languages without a human narrator.

5. **Automated Video Scriptwriting**: Use **ShortlyAI** or **Sudowrite** to craft engaging scripts for YouTube videos or commercials, reducing the time spent on content development.

6. **Custom AI Music Production**: Employ **AIVA**, an AI music composition tool, to create original soundtracks or background music for videos, podcasts, or digital content without needing musical expertise.

7. **Educational Content and Tutorials**: Develop comprehensive educational content or tutorials for online courses or YouTube educational channels with **Quizlet's AI features**, personalized to different learning styles and subjects.

8. **Automated Social Media Content**: Implement **Lately's AI-powered social media tool** to auto-generate social media posts from longer content pieces, ensuring a consistent and engaging online presence.

9. **Dynamic Email Campaigns**: Use **Persado** to optimize email marketing campaigns with AI-generated language that resonates best with your audience, improving open rates and conversions.

10. **AI-Assisted Film and Animation Creation**: Explore **Runway ML** for editing and creating film content,

using AI to automate tasks like object removal, scene composition, or even generating animated sequences.

These ideas demonstrate the breadth of possibilities when integrating LLMs into various content-creation processes. By harnessing these tools, creators and businesses can significantly enhance productivity, creativity, and engagement with their target audiences.

Strategies for Passive Income with AI

- **Content Creation and Monetization**: Utilize AI writing tools such as **Jasper AI** for blog posts and articles. For video content, **Lumen5** and **Runway ML** can assist in creating engaging videos. Monetize this content through platforms like YouTube, blogs, or selling digital products.
- **Affiliate Marketing Optimization**: Employ AI tools like **Affise** to analyze and optimize affiliate marketing strategies, enhancing the effectiveness of marketing efforts with minimal manual intervention.
- **Automated E-commerce**: Use AI platforms like **Shopify**, integrated with tools such as **ChatGPT** for customer service, to automate and personalize the shopping experience, boosting sales with minimal ongoing management.
- **AI-Powered Investment and Trading**: Leverage AI for predictive modeling in financial markets with tools like **Wealthfront** or **Betterment** for personal investments or offer AI-driven advisory services.
- **AI in Education and Training**: Create AI-personalized learning experiences with platforms like **Thinkific**, using AI to curate content and sell online courses.

Innovative AI-Enabled Income Streams:

- **AI-Generated Art and Design**: Use tools like **DALL-E,** and **Midjourney** for creating unique artwork and **Canva's**

Magic Write for designing, which can be sold as digital products.

- **Voice Generation and Podcasting**: Tools such as **Descript** allow for creating podcasts or voiceovers for videos with AI-generated voices.
- **Language Translation Services**: Utilize AI for offering translation services, expanding the reach of content across global markets.
- **AI-Driven Consultation Services**: Offer consultancy in various niches, leveraging AI for data analysis to provide insights.
- **Developing AI-Powered Apps and Games**: With platforms like **Unity**, integrate AI to create unique gaming experiences or utility apps.

Avoiding Common Pitfalls

Success in generating passive income with AI requires awareness of common pitfalls, such as overreliance on AI without understanding the basics, choosing overly complex tools, ignoring compatibility with existing systems, and neglecting regular updates and maintenance of AI tools.

Moving Forward

Leveraging AI for passive income can be a lucrative business venture if you understand the basics, select the right AI tools, and continuously learn and adapt.

This streamlined approach focuses on a variety of AI-enabled strategies for passive income, removing redundancies and providing a concise guide to harnessing AI's potential from home.

3.2: AI-DRIVEN AFFILIATE MARKETING: A BEGINNER'S GUIDE

Affiliate Marketing Explained

Affiliate marketing is a digital marketing strategy commonly used. It offers the opportunity to receive a commission by promoting products or services and persuading individuals to complete a sale or specific action through your referral. Affiliate marketing is a popular passive income stream because it can generate earnings with minimal ongoing effort, especially when enhanced with AI technologies.

Using AI to Identify Opportunities

AI tools are revolutionizing affiliate marketing by analyzing market trends and consumer behavior to identify lucrative niches and products. Tools like **Jasper** can assist in content creation by providing keyword-rich, engaging articles that rank well in search engines and attract potential buyers.

Automating Affiliate Marketing Tasks

AI can automate various tasks in affiliate marketing, from generating content to tracking link performance and analyzing the effectiveness of marketing strategies. **Adscook** and **Scaleo** are examples of AI-driven platforms that optimize ad campaigns and affiliate marketing efforts, offering easy-to-understand analytics, fraud detection, and real-time performance optimization.

Success Stories and Best Practices

The integration of AI into affiliate marketing has led to numerous success stories. Amazon and Airbnb have successfully utilized AI to analyze the behavior of their customers, enabling them to personalize campaigns that have led to higher conversions and more significant revenue. Adopting AI for affiliate marketing involves starting with the right tools, tracking and analyzing results, being flexible, and staying updated on AI advancements.

Best practices for integrating AI into your affiliate marketing strategy include starting small, testing various AI tools, closely tracking results, being adaptable, and continuously educating yourself on new AI technologies and trends.

For a deeper understanding of leveraging AI in affiliate marketing, beginners can refer to these resources with their entire website addresses:

- **Jasper.ai** offers tools for content creation and enhancing affiliate marketing efforts with AI-driven insights and optimization. More details can be found at https://www.jasper.ai.

- **Scaleo** is an AI-powered affiliate marketing platform that provides tracking, optimization, and fraud detection. Discover more at https://www.scaleo.io.
- **Pepper Content** discusses the benefits of AI in affiliate marketing, from identifying profitable niches to optimizing campaigns for better sales. Learn more at https://www.peppercontent.io.

These references offer a blend of theoretical knowledge and practical applications of AI in affiliate marketing, guiding beginners through the process of automating and enhancing their affiliate marketing strategies.

3.3: BUILDING AND SELLING AI-CREATED DIGITAL PRODUCTS

Types of AI-Created Digital Products

AI technologies offer creative avenues for generating digital products, including:

- **eBooks**: Leveraging AI to compile and write informative content on various topics.
- **Art**: Utilizing AI art generators like **Midjourney** or **DALL-E** to create unique visual content.
- **Music**: Employing AI music generators such as **AIVA** for composing original music tracks.
- **Software Tools**: Developing AI-based applications that solve specific problems or enhance productivity.

Creating Digital Products with AI Tools

Creating high-quality digital products involves several steps:

1. **Selecting the Right AI Tool**: Choose an AI tool that aligns with the type of digital product you intend to create, considering factors like ease of use and output quality.

2. **Refining Output**: Use the AI tool to generate the initial product, then refine the output to ensure originality, add personal touches, and increase the overall value.

Marketing and Selling Your Products

Successfully marketing and selling AI-created digital products involves:

- **Pricing Strategy**: Set competitive prices that reflect the value of your product.
- **Distribution Channels**: Utilize online platforms such as **Etsy** for art, **Amazon Kindle Direct Publishing** for eBooks, and **Bandcamp** or **SoundCloud** for music.
- **Customer Engagement**: Engage with your audience and create a community focused on your products by utilizing both social media and email marketing.

Legal and Ethical Considerations

When selling AI-created digital products, it's crucial to navigate legal and ethical waters carefully:

- **Copyright Compliance**: Ensure your AI-generated content complies with copyright laws, especially when using pre-existing data or models.
- **Transparency**: Be transparent about using AI to create your products, which can foster trust with your customers.
- **User Consent**: If your product collects user data, ensure you have consent and adhere to privacy regulations.

Resources and Tools:

- **Heights Platform's blog** provides insights into AI-generated digital products you can start selling online today, highlighting tools like **Adobe Firefly** and **Midjourney** for digital art creation.

- **Generativeai.pub** shares firsthand experiences of selling AI designs on Etsy, offering practical tips for using AI tools to create digital downloads.
- **Aipowerlab.io** lists digital products to create and sell, such as voiceovers generated by **Murf.ai** and music tracks with **Soundraw.io**.

3.4: USING AI TO ENHANCE E-COMMERCE SALES

AI in E-commerce Overview

AI plays a crucial role in enhancing e-commerce operations, streamlining everything from personalized recommendations to efficient inventory management. By analyzing customer behavior and preferences, AI technologies offer personalized shopping experiences, thereby boosting customer engagement and sales.

Boosting Sales with AI

AI technologies aid in boosting e-commerce sales through:

- **Personalized Recommendations**: This involves analyzing past purchases and browsing behavior to tailor product suggestions, similar to Amazon's use of collaborative filtering to enhance its recommendation system.
- **Dynamic Pricing**: Using AI, prices can be adjusted in real time, considering factors like demand and competitor pricing. This ensures that the business stays competitive and optimizes its margins.
- **Chatbots for Customer Service**: Implementing AI-powered chatbots to handle customer inquiries round the clock, enhancing customer service and engagement, as seen with Alibaba and eBay using NLP for product recommendations.

Case Studies of Successful AI Integration

- **Amazon**: Uses AI for personalized product recommendations, significantly impacting sales and customer loyalty by accurately predicting customer needs.

- **JD.com**: Automation technologies improved warehouse operations and delivery efficiency, leading to faster order processing and enhanced customer satisfaction.
- **Shopify**: AI systems scale automatically during high-traffic events like Black Friday to handle the increased load, ensuring a smooth customer experience.

Tools and Platforms for AI E-commerce

For e-commerce businesses looking to integrate AI, several tools and platforms stand out:

- **Shopify Sidekick**: A generative AI bot assisting online store owners with various tasks, from setting up discounts to summarizing sales data.
- **ChatGPT by OpenAI**: This can be customized for e-commerce applications, providing conversational agents for shopping and customer support.
- **Salesforce Einstein**: This AI-powered tool amplifies CRM with smart features for sales predictions, customer insights, and automated marketing strategies, making it a valuable asset for e-commerce businesses seeking growth.

In addition to the AI e-commerce examples already discussed, here are three more to consider, demonstrating the breadth of AI applications in enhancing online retail experiences:

- **Zara**: Zara has employed AI to optimize its inventory management system. By analyzing sales data and customer preferences, Zara ensures popular items are restocked efficiently, reducing overstock and understock situations. This strategic use of AI keeps their offerings fresh and high in customer satisfaction.
- **Netflix**: While primarily a streaming service, Netflix's use of AI for personalized content recommendations offers lessons for e-commerce. By analyzing viewing habits, Netflix presents users with tailored options, increasing engagement. Products can be suggested for e-

commerce based on customers' browsing and purchase
history.
- **Sephora**: Sephora's Virtual Artist app uses augmented
  reality and AI to allow customers to try makeup virtually
  before buying. This innovative use of technology has
  significantly improved the online shopping experience,
  leading to higher conversion rates and customer satisfaction.

These examples highlight how AI can be leveraged across different
aspects of e-commerce to improve inventory management, personalize
customer experiences, and enhance product discovery and trial, ultimately driving sales and customer loyalty.

For a deeper dive into the integration of AI in e-commerce and to
explore these examples further, the following resources provide
comprehensive insights and case studies:

- Master of Code discusses AI's impact on e-commerce,
  including chatbots and personalized shopping experiences.
  Accessed at: https://masterofcode.com.
- McKinsey offers insights into how AI technologies are
  transforming the retail landscape, including inventory
  management and customer engagement strategies. Available
  at: https://www.mckinsey.com.
- DZone explores various AI applications in e-commerce, from
  dynamic pricing to customer service enhancements. Find out
  more at: https://dzone.com.
- Emerj provides detailed case studies on successful AI
  integrations in e-commerce, showcasing companies like
  JD.com and Amazon. Read more at: https://emerj.com.
- Flatlogic Blog covers top AI tools for e-commerce, including
  real-life examples of AI-driven success stories.
  Visit https://flatlogic.com.

These resources offer valuable perspectives on utilizing AI to
enhance e-commerce operations, from back-end logistics to front-end
customer interactions, demonstrating the potential of AI to revolutionize the retail industry.

3.5: CREATING AI-GENERATED CONTENT FOR MONETIZATION

Monetizing AI-Generated Content

AI-generated content offers a unique opportunity for monetization across various platforms, including blogs, videos, and podcasts. The key to monetization lies in creating content that engages and provides value to your audience. Utilizing AI technology, it's possible to generate content that is of high quality and consistent in nature. This content has the potential to resonate well with your target audience, which in turn provides opportunities to generate revenue through methods such as ads, subscriptions, and others.

Tools for AI Content Creation

Several AI tools have revolutionized content creation by making it more efficient and accessible. ChatGPT, for example, is rapidly becoming a go-to for generating written content, speeding up the research process, and helping draft content briefs and layouts. Long-Shot offers services for social media and blog writing, with features like headline generators and content rephrasing. For sourcing and referencing, Perplexity is an advanced AI writing tool that enriches content with credible sources, ensuring the produced material is authoritative and well-grounded.

Descript brings innovation to podcasting and video content with its Overdub feature, which creates ultra-realistic human voice clones, allowing for a broad range of content creation possibilities without the need for extensive recording equipment or acting talent.

Maintaining Quality and Authenticity

While AI tools can significantly aid in content creation, maintaining quality and authenticity is paramount. This involves a hybrid approach, where AI-generated content is blended with human creativity and oversight to ensure originality and align with audience expectations. It's crucial to review and refine AI-generated content to maintain a human touch, ensuring it resonates with your audience on a personal level.

Examples of Successful AI Content Monetization

The digital art field, for instance, has seen significant growth in AI-generated content. Artists can now use advanced platforms such as

DALL-E and PixelPainter to create exclusive artwork that challenges the limits of conventional art, providing fresh opportunities for earning money through the sale of digital art and commissions.Wirestock.io highlights the potential of selling AI artwork, provided it's original and doesn't infringe on existing copyrights.

Moreover, Mighty Networks offers insights into content monetization strategies beyond direct sales, such as leveraging subscriptions, paywalls, and affiliate marketing, each with its own pros and cons. These strategies underscore the diverse ways AI-generated content can be monetized, emphasizing the importance of choosing the right model based on your content type and audience.

For more in-depth strategies and examples on creating and monetizing AI-generated content, you can explore resources provided by ContentStudio, Wirestock, and Mighty Networks at their respective websites:

- ContentStudio Blog: https://blog.contentstudio.io
- Wirestock Blog: https://blog.wirestock.io
- Mighty Networks: https://www.mightynetworks.com

In addition to the AI content creation tools mentioned, here are five more that can significantly enhance your ability to produce and monetize digital content:

1. **Canva**: While known for its design capabilities, Canva also offers features powered by AI, such as text generation for social media posts and marketing materials. It's particularly useful for creating visually appealing content quickly. Explore more at Canva's website.
2. **Artbreeder**: Artbreeder uses generative adversarial networks (GANs) to allow users to create unique images by blending existing photos. It's trendy for creating AI-generated art and character designs for monetization. Check it out at Artbreeder's website.
3. **Copy.ai**: Copy.ai leverages AI to help you write better marketing copy, blog posts, and even product descriptions. It's designed to save time on content creation by providing

high-quality drafts that you can refine and personalize.
Learn more at Copy.ai's website.

4. **Synthesia**: Synthesia creates AI-driven video content from text, enabling the production of engaging videos without the need for actors or complex video equipment. It's useful for creating tutorials, courses, and promotional videos. Visit Synthesia's website for more information.

5. **Zyro**: Zyro offers AI-powered website-building tools, including blog content generation, product descriptions, and more. It's a great resource for anyone looking to launch an e-commerce site or online portfolio with minimal effort. Find out more at Zyro's website.

6. **Rytr** is an AI writing assistant that generates content across multiple formats, including blogs, emails, and social media posts. It uses natural language processing to create engaging content tailored to your specific needs. Find out more at https://rytr.me.

7. **Lobe**: Lobe by Microsoft enables the creation, training, and deployment of personalized deep learning models without any coding efforts. It's particularly useful for creators and developers looking to incorporate AI functionalities into their applications or services at https://lobe.ai.

8. **DeepL Translator**: DeepL utilizes state-of-the-art AI and machine learning technology to provide exceptional translation services. Its accuracy is highly reliable, making it an excellent choice for individuals and businesses who wish to communicate with a global audience by translating their content into multiple languages https://www.deepl.com/translator.

9. **Pictory**: This tool uses AI to convert long-form content into engaging short videos, which is ideal for content marketing on social media platforms. Pictory can analyze a script and automatically select relevant visuals, making video production faster and more efficient at https://pictory.ai.

10. **Chatsonic by Writesonic**: Similar to ChatGPT, Chatsonic generates text-based content, supports voice commands, and can generate images. It's designed for creating interactive

and multimedia content, from detailed articles to graphic designs and more. Visit https://writesonic.com/chatsonic to learn more.

These tools showcase the diversity of AI applications in content creation, from writing and translation to video production and interactive media, offering creators innovative ways to engage with their audience and streamline their workflows. By leveraging AI, you can streamline the creative process, maintain a high level of quality and originality in your work, and explore new opportunities for generating income online.

3.6 AUTOMATING ONLINE COURSES WITH AI

The Potential of AI in Online Education

Artificial Intelligence (AI) holds the promise of transforming the landscape of online education by introducing personalized learning paths, automated grading systems, and interactive and immersive learning experiences. With AI, educators can create tailored educational content that adapts to each student's learning style, thereby enhancing student engagement and improving knowledge retention. AI's ability to provide adaptive assessments and feedback, coupled with intelligent content recommendations, opens up new avenues for personalized education that can cater to the unique needs of each learner.

Creating AI-Powered Online Courses

To harness the power of AI in online education, educators must start by integrating AI technologies that can automate content delivery and facilitate dynamic interactions with students. This involves developing a curriculum that leverages AI tools for creating interactive content, such as simulations and quizzes, which adapt based on the learner's performance. Additionally, educators can utilize AI to analyze learning data in real time, enabling them to adjust the course content and teaching strategies to better meet students' needs. Educators can create a more engaging and effective learning environment by incorporating AI-powered virtual tutors and utilizing platforms that support automated content generation.

Marketing Your AI-Powered Courses

To effectively market AI-powered online courses, it's crucial to highlight AI's unique benefits to the learning experience. This includes emphasizing personalized learning paths, the convenience of self-paced study, and the innovative use of technology to enhance educational outcomes. Marketing strategies should focus on showcasing the effectiveness of AI in improving knowledge retention and engaging learners through interactive content. Leveraging social media, educational forums, and e-learning platforms to share success stories and testimonials can also help attract potential learners to AI-powered courses.

Feedback and Improvement with AI

AI technology is instrumental in collecting and analyzing student feedback, which can be used to continuously improve online courses. By employing AI tools that track learning patterns and assess student satisfaction, educators can identify areas of the course that may require adjustments or enhancements. AI's ability to quickly analyze large volumes of data means that course creators can swiftly implement changes based on actionable insights, ensuring content remains relevant and effective. Moreover, AI can facilitate the creation of a feedback loop where students' interactions with the course material are continuously monitored and used to refine the learning experience.

Here are ten AI tools that can help automate various aspects of online courses, from content creation to grading and personalized learning experiences:

1. **Coursera Lab**: Offers an environment for creating and delivering courses with AI-powered tools for content personalization and interactive learning experiences. It helps in automating the grading system and providing personalized feedback to students.

2. **Quizlet**: Quizlet is a platform famous for its learning flashcards. It uses AI to generate personalized study sets and practice tests. This feature helps students learn at their desired pace and keep track of their progress at https://quizlet.com.

3. **ScribeSense**: An AI tool that automates grading for handwritten and digital assignments. It's beneficial for teachers who want to save time on grading and focus more on teaching.

4. **Duolingo**: Uses AI to offer personalized language learning experiences. Its AI algorithms adapt the content based on the learner's performance, providing custom lessons that fit the individual's learning pace. Visit https://www.duolingo.com

5. **Carnegie Learning**: A platform that provides AI-powered math learning tools. It personalizes learning experiences for students, offering real-time feedback and adaptive learning paths. https://www.carnegielearning.com.

6. **Knewton Alta**: An adaptive learning technology that provides personalized learning experiences for higher education. The difficulty level of the material is adjusted based on the student's performance using AI; check https://www.knewton.com

7. **Content Technologies, Inc. (CTI)**: Uses AI to create custom textbooks and learning materials. This tool can compile content based on specific course requirements, helping educators to provide tailored resources.

8. **Grammarly**: While primarily a writing assistant, Grammarly uses AI to help students improve their writing skills, offering real-time grammar, punctuation, and style suggestions. It's beneficial for essay assignments and peer feedback sessions. Access https://www.grammarly.com

9. **ALEKS**: An adaptive learning platform from McGraw-Hill that uses AI to identify students' knowledge and learning gaps. It then creates personalized learning paths to guide them to mastery in subjects like math, chemistry, and accounting. Visit https://www.aleks.com

10. **IBM Watson Education**: Offers a range of AI-powered tools to support personalized learning and analytics. It can analyze students' learning habits and performance, providing insights to educators for better instructional strategies. https://www.ibm.com/industries/education

In conclusion, AI tools have emerged as powerful allies in the pursuit of multiple passive income streams, offering unparalleled efficiency and innovation. By automating routine tasks, AI allows individuals to focus on strategy and creativity, significantly enhancing productivity. The versatility and scalability of AI tools empower individuals to diversify their income sources with ease. Whether through content creation, e-commerce, digital design, or investment automation, AI opens the door to numerous passive income opportunities, enabling a more sustainable and financially independent lifestyle. As AI technology continues to evolve, the potential for creating and managing passive income streams will only expand, making it an indispensable resource for modern entrepreneurs.

CHAPTER 4

TRANSFORM CLICKS INTO CURRENCY

4.1 UNDERSTANDING AI IN DIGITAL MARKETING: AN OVERVIEW

In the constantly shifting realm of digital marketing, Artificial Intelligence (AI) has become a game-changing element, transforming how brands engage with their audience. This chapter explores the integration and benefits of AI in digital marketing strategies, drawing upon various sources to provide a comprehensive overview.

- **The Role of AI in Modern Marketing**: AI's application in digital marketing is expansive, facilitating personalized and data-driven campaigns that engage customers more effectively than ever. Technologies like machine learning, predictive analytics, and natural language processing equip marketers with the tools to parse through vast amounts of data, predict upcoming trends, and create content that establishes a personal connection with their audience.
- **Benefits of AI-Driven Marketing**: Leveraging AI in marketing strategies has significant advantages. These include enhanced customer insights through data analysis, higher engagement rates with personalized content, and increased ROI from optimized campaign strategies. AI's

predictive capabilities also allow for more accurate targeting and segmentation.

- **AI Technologies in Marketing**: Key AI technologies employed in marketing include machine learning for pattern recognition and predictive analytics, natural language processing for content creation and customer service automation, and AI-driven chatbots for instant customer interaction. Each technology is critical in automating and optimizing various facets of digital marketing.
- **Integrating AI into Your Marketing Strategy**: Incorporating AI into a marketing strategy involves identifying areas where AI can add value, like data analysis, content creation, or customer service. The process includes selecting appropriate AI tools, integrating them with existing platforms, and continually monitoring and optimizing their performance to ensure maximum impact.

For those looking to delve deeper into the practical application of AI in digital marketing, various AI tools have been highlighted across sources:

- **Content Creation and Optimization Tools**: MarketMuse, ChatGPT, and Copy.ai are notable for their abilities to generate and optimize content, ensuring it is both engaging for the audience and favorable for search engine rankings.
- **AI Chatbots for Customer Engagement**: Tools like Chatfuel and ManyChat facilitate automated customer interactions, providing personalized responses and enhancing the customer experience.
- **Video Creation and Voice Generation**: Synthesia and Murf offer innovative solutions for creating videos and voiceovers with AI, enabling marketers to produce high-quality content efficiently.
- **Predictive Analytics and SEO**: Tools like Frase.io and Surfer SEO help optimize content and strategy based on predictive analytics and SEO insights, improving visibility and engagement.

4.2 PERSONALIZING CUSTOMER EXPERIENCES WITH AI

In the dynamic landscape of digital marketing, personalizing customer experiences has become paramount. Artificial Intelligence (AI) is at the forefront of this transformation, equipping marketers with sophisticated tools to comprehend and connect with their customers more intimately.

- **Understanding Customer Data**: At the heart of AI-enhanced customization is the acquisition and examination of consumer data. AI tools are capable of examining vast arrays of data points to uncover patterns, preferences, and behaviors that go beyond traditional demographics. This allows businesses to develop highly customized marketing strategies, ensuring an unparalleled customer experience.
- **Segmentation and Targeting with AI**: AI enhances the ability to segment audiences with precision, utilizing machine learning algorithms to analyze customer journeys, behaviors, and transactions. This facilitates the delivery of tailored recommendations, akin to how Netflix personalizes viewing experiences for its users.
- **Customizing Content with AI**: AI's role extends to content customization, where it can generate or modify content to suit the preferences of different audience segments. Dotdigital, for example, leverages AI to offer personalized product recommendations, optimizing engagement at various stages of the customer journey.
- **Measuring the Impact of Personalization**: AI tools also offer advanced metrics and predictive analytics to gauge the effectiveness of personalized marketing efforts. These include the ability to forecast future customer behaviors and preferences, providing a clear picture of personalization's impact on marketing success.

For businesses looking to enhance their customer experience through personalization, here are five AI tools that can help:

1. **Customerly**: An AI-based customer support platform offering round-the-clock assistance and marketing automation capabilities.
2. **VoiceGenie**: A generative AI-powered voice bot that supports over 100 languages and dialects.
3. **Intellimize**: A platform for personalizing marketing website experiences across the customer journey.
4. **Adobe Target**: Utilizes AI to personalize experiences across web, mobile, and applications with A/B and multivariate testing.
5. **Fabriq**: BCG's AI-powered marketing personalization platform that assists in knowing, acquiring, and nurturing customer relationships.

These tools underscore the transformative potential of AI in crafting personalized customer experiences that resonate on an individual level. By leveraging AI, companies can ensure their marketing strategies are efficient and highly pertinent to their target audience.

4.3 AI-POWERED CONTENT CREATION: BLOGGING TO VLOGGING

The world of content creation is experiencing a profound transformation thanks to the introduction of Artificial Intelligence (AI), which is changing how we craft and oversee digital content. From blogging to vlogging, AI tools are reshaping the content landscape, offering innovative solutions for creators across the spectrum.

- **Automating Content Creation**: AI tools like ClickUp, Narrato, and Jasper are revolutionizing the content creation process. ClickUp, for instance, offers a comprehensive project management platform with an AI content writing assistant that facilitates brainstorming, copyediting, and summarizing extensive texts. Jasper, renowned for its ability to generate a wide array of content, including blog posts, e-books, and social media posts, stands out for its user-friendly templates and Brand Voice feature, which ensures content coherence.

- **Enhancing Content Quality with AI**: AI doesn't just streamline content creation; it also enhances its quality. For example, Writesonic and Kafkai are tools designed to assist in generating high-quality, SEO-friendly content. Writesonic, built on GPT-4 technology, offers over 100 features like plagiarism checkers and keyword extractors to ensure your content is both original and optimized.

- **Scaling Content Production with AI**: Scaling content doesn't have to mean a drop in quality. AI tools enable the mass production of personalized, high-quality content. For instance, Descript and Synthesia offer unique solutions for podcasters, YouTubers, and online educators by simplifying the editing process and creating realistic avatars for video content, making it easier to scale without sacrificing quality or authenticity.

- **Content Management and Distribution**: Managing and distributing content efficiently across multiple channels can be daunting. AI tools streamline these processes, ensuring that your content reaches the right audience at the right time. For instance, Canva's AI image generator helps create visually appealing social media content, enhancing both the management and distribution of digital content.

For those looking to dive deeper into the world of AI-powered content creation, these tools provide a starting point:

1. **ClickUp**: A versatile project management tool with built-in AI content creation features.
2. **Jasper**: Offers a wide range of templates and a Brand Voice feature for cohesive content creation.
3. **Writesonic**: Utilizes GPT-4 technology for content generation across various marketing materials.
4. **Descript**: Simplifies podcast and video production with AI-driven editing tools.

5. **Synthesia**: Creates realistic avatars for video content, offering a novel solution for digital educators and marketers.

4.4 MASTERING AI FOR SEO: STRATEGIES THAT WORK

Leveraging Artificial Intelligence (AI) in SEO is revolutionizing our approach to search engine optimization, making processes more streamlined and outcomes more impactful. Here's a look at how AI can enhance various aspects of your SEO strategy:

- **AI in Keyword Research and Optimization**: AI tools like Semrush and Outranking are pivotal in uncovering high-performing keywords and optimizing content to boost search engine visibility. Semrush, for instance, excels in content optimization and readability improvements, while Outranking aids in creating detailed content briefs and automating SEO tasks like internal linking.
- **Improving On-Page SEO with AI**: On-page SEO elements—meta tags, headings, image alt texts—are crucial for rankings. AI platforms such as Alli AI and Outranking can automate optimizing these elements. Alli AI, for example, offers solutions for on-page optimizations and site speed improvements, streamlining SEO efforts.
- **Backlink Analysis and Optimization with AI**: Analyzing backlink profiles and identifying link-building opportunities can significantly impact site authority. Tools like Alli AI provide insights by examining large websites and suggesting potential links, thus facilitating the link-building process.
- **Monitoring SEO Performance with AI Tools**: Monitoring your SEO performance is essential for understanding and enhancing your strategy. AI tools such as SE Ranking and GrowthBar offer features for tracking changes in content, auditing website performance, and monitoring keyword rankings, offering a comprehensive overview of your SEO health.

For businesses looking to leverage AI for SEO, the following tools provide a solid foundation:

1. **Semrush**: Offers a vast array of features including content auditing and AI-generated content, integrated with major platforms like Google Docs and WordPress(Semrush).
2. **Outranking**: Known for its content optimization features and the ability to automate many SEO tasks(Outranking).
3. **Alli AI**: A versatile tool for on-page optimizations and SEO testing, capable of automating meta tags and internal linking (Alli AI).
4. **SE Ranking**: Monitors page changes and provides a comprehensive website audit tool, though it comes with additional costs for full features (SE Ranking).
5. **GrowthBar**: Ideal for content teams, offering a blog ideas generator and post outline builder(GrowthBar).

Integrating AI into your SEO strategy streamlines processes and offers insights and optimizations that might not be apparent through manual analysis alone. These tools represent the cutting edge of SEO technology, enabling businesses to enhance their online visibility and drive more organic traffic effectively.

4.5 SOCIAL MEDIA AND AI: ENGAGING YOUR AUDIENCE

Integrating Artificial Intelligence into social media strategies revolutionizes how brands engage with their audience. Here's how AI can enhance your social media presence:

- **AI for Social Media Analysis**: AI tools like Brandwatch and Acrolinx offer profound insights into social media trends and audience behavior, enabling brands to tailor their content and engagement strategies more effectively. Brandwatch excels in analyzing data at scale to provide AI-created insights and statistics, while Acrolinx ensures content aligns with your brand voice, improving consistency and engagement.

- **Automating Social Media Interactions**: Conversational AI chatbots, such as Heyday by Hootsuite, facilitate 24/7 customer service, handling inquiries and enhancing engagement on social media platforms. These AI-powered tools can deliver personalized interactions, significantly boosting e-commerce sales and customer satisfaction rates.
- **Content Optimization for Social Media**: Platforms like Canva and Let's Enhance utilize AI to automate and optimize content creation for social posts, presentations, and videos. Canva simplifies content creation with AI-assisted design tools, while Let's Enhance improves image quality by creating visually compelling content that resonates with your audience.
- **Influencer Partnership and AI**: Identifying the right influencer partnerships is crucial for brand alignment and audience engagement. AI tools can analyze vast amounts of data to recommend influencers whose followers match your target demographic, optimizing your influencer marketing strategy.

If you're a social media manager or content creator thinking about using AI to up your game, here are some standout tools you should consider:

1. **FeedHive**: Streamlines content scheduling and automates posting, ensuring a consistent online presence.
2. **Vista Social**: Allows easy management across numerous social media channels, simplifying multi-platform strategies.
3. **Buffer**: Tailors posts for each social media channel, enhancing content relevance and engagement.
4. **Flick**: Converts single content ideas into multiple posts, maximizing content production efficiency.
5. **Audiense**: Provides intelligent social listening on Twitter, offering insights into audience preferences and trends.

6. **Ocoya**: Assists in writing captions and hashtags, optimizing content for search and engagement.
7. **Predis.ai**: Generates engaging carousels and videos, enhancing visual content strategy.
8. **ClickUp AI**: Supports a variety of content creation tasks, from campaign strategy to social post copy, streamlining the content creation process.
9. **SocialBee**: An all-in-one social media management tool that automates post-generation and scheduling, making content management more efficient.

These AI tools streamline workflow, enhance content creation, and provide actionable insights for a more strategic and engaging online presence. By incorporating AI into your social media strategy, you can achieve greater reach, engagement, and a stronger connection with your audience.

4.6 EMAIL MARKETING REVOLUTIONIZED BY AI

Email marketing remains a critical tool for businesses seeking to connect with their audience in this digital age. In this chapter, we will discuss how AI has revolutionized email marketing. The focus will be on AI-powered email personalization and how it drives better engagement metrics like open and click-through rates.

AI-Driven Email Personalization

At the core of AI's transformative power in email marketing is its ability to tailor content to the individual level, offering a level of personalization previously unattainable. This section delves into how AI facilitates this personalization and the benefits it brings.

- **Understanding AI Personalization:** In email marketing, AI personalization involves using machine learning algorithms to assess a recipient's conduct, inclinations, and interaction history. This data is then used to customize every aspect of an email, from subject lines to content and product recommendations, ensuring that each communication feels uniquely relevant to the recipient.

- **The Mechanics of Personalization:** AI systems collect and analyze data from various touchpoints, including website interactions, purchase history, and email engagement. By identifying patterns and preferences within this data, AI can predict which products a customer might be interested in or the type of content that will engage them the most. This information is used to create highly targeted and personalized email campaigns.
- **Impact on Open and Click-Through Rates:** Personalizing email content and subject lines significantly enhances the likelihood of emails being opened and interacted with. Emails personalized to the recipient's specific needs and interests tend to have higher open and click-through rates, as they are more likely to grab the recipient's attention and encourage engagement. When this approach is used, email marketing campaigns become more effective, and the bond between brands and their customers gets stronger.
- **Success Stories:** Many businesses have reported remarkable improvements in their marketing metrics after implementing AI-driven personalization strategies. These success stories often highlight double-digit increases in open rates and significant uplifts in click-through and conversion rates, underscoring the effectiveness of personalized content.
- **Getting Started with AI Personalization:** The first step is to integrate AI-enabled email marketing platforms for businesses looking to harness the power of AI-driven email personalization. These platforms offer tools and features that automate the data analysis and personalization process, making it easier for marketers to create compelling, personalized email campaigns.

Optimizing Send Times with AI

In the quest to maximize email engagement, the timing of your email can be as crucial as its content. Artificial Intelligence (AI) offers a sophisticated solution to this challenge by analyzing recipient behavior to determine the optimal times for sending emails. This process involves:

- **Behavioral Analysis:** AI algorithms scrutinize past engagement data, such as open and click-through rates, to identify patterns in recipient behavior. This data-driven approach ensures that emails are sent when recipients are most likely to engage.
- **Adaptive Learning:** Unlike static scheduling strategies, AI continually refines its predictions based on ongoing recipient interactions, ensuring that the timing of emails evolves with changing behavior patterns.
- **Personalization at Scale:** AI enables the personalization of send times at an individual level, accommodating the diverse routines and preferences within an email list. This individualized approach significantly boosts the chances of emails being opened and read.

Email Campaign Analysis

The potential of AI goes beyond just optimizing the timing of email campaigns; it also has a crucial role in assessing their performance. This involves:

- **Performance Metrics:** AI tools can analyze campaign data for performance insights, such as open rates, click-through rates, and conversion rates.
- **Success Elements Identification:** Through the analysis, AI can pinpoint which elements of an email campaign resonate with the audience, from subject lines to content and call-to-action buttons.
- **Adjustment Recommendations:** By identifying areas for improvement, AI can suggest actionable adjustments, helping marketers refine their strategies for better outcomes.

Segmentation and Automation

The power of AI in email marketing also extends to segmentation and automation, enhancing both efficiency and effectiveness:

- **Dynamic Segmentation:** By analyzing user data such as behavior, preferences, and purchase history, AI algorithms can create highly targeted groups to segment email lists more accurately. This segmentation method enables AI-powered assistants to generate more personalized email campaigns geared towards specific groups.

- **Automated Campaign Workflows:** AI can automate the entire email campaign process, from sending personalized emails based on user actions to adjusting campaign parameters in real time for optimized performance.

Examples of AI Tools for Email Marketing

1. **ActiveCampaign:** Offers advanced segmentation, personalized content, and automation capabilities.
2. **Mailchimp:** Known for its predictive segmentation and customized product recommendations.
3. **Campaign Monitor:** Utilizes AI for optimizing send times and improving email campaign performance.
4. **Sendinblue:** Features AI algorithms for send-time optimization and behavioral-targeted emails.
5. **Moosend:** Provides AI-powered automation workflows and audience segmentation.

Integrating AI into email marketing represents a significant leap forward, transforming a one-size-fits-all communication method into a highly personalized and engaging experience. As AI technology continues to evolve, the possibilities for innovative and effective email marketing strategies will expand, offering businesses unprecedented opportunities to connect with their audiences in meaningful ways. The era of AI-driven email personalization is just beginning, promising a future where email marketing is not just practical but genuinely exciting for recipients.

4.7 CHATBOTS AND CUSTOMER SERVICE: AI FOR ENHANCED INTERACTIONS

Using AI chatbots in customer service transforms how companies engage with their clients. These advanced tools offer 24/7 assistance, streamlining interactions and enhancing user satisfaction. Here's how to effectively implement and utilize AI chatbots for customer service.

Implementing AI Chatbots

To deploy AI chatbots on websites and social media platforms, select a tool that aligns with your business needs. Options like Ultimate and Zendesk bots offer no-code platforms and intuitive Dialogue Builders, making it simple for customer support teams to develop advanced conversation flows. Ultimate excels in understanding short, informal customer service messages without a translation layer, ensuring support in 109 languages. Zendesk bots, on the other hand, are tailored to guide customers to knowledge-based articles and enhance self-service options.

Customizing Chatbot Interactions

Customization is key to reflecting your brand's voice and effectively meeting customer needs. Tools like Netomi and Freddy AI allow businesses to customize chatbots extensively. Netomi supports conversational responses across multiple platforms, while Freddy AI, designed by Freshworks, automates solutions to common queries in numerous languages. These platforms learn from your knowledge base and FAQs, ensuring chatbots improve over time.

Integrating Chatbots with CRM Systems

Integrate your chatbot with CRM systems for personalized interactions based on customer history and preferences. Platforms like Bitrix24 and Intercom facilitate this integration, enhancing customer service and engagement. Bitrix24 provides a comprehensive suite for collaboration and CRM, including superior communication tools and seamless integration capabilities. Intercom, known for reliable and efficient customer engagement, offers a swift setup and a range of customization options.

Measuring Chatbot Success

Leverage advanced analytics and reporting features available in many AI chatbot platforms to gauge the effectiveness of chatbot interactions. Assess metrics related to customer satisfaction, resolution time, and sales impact. Tools like Dixa and Salesforce offer detailed insights into chatbot performance, helping businesses continually refine their customer service approach.

For businesses considering implementing AI chatbots, exploring these tools and strategies can significantly enhance customer service operations, providing a seamless and efficient experience for both customers and service teams.

ManyChat is a leading chat automation platform for creating chatbots on Facebook, Instagram, WhatsApp, and SMS. It's user-friendly with a visual flow builder, allowing easy chatbot creation without coding. ManyChat offers free and paid plans starting at $15/month, making it accessible for businesses of all sizes to engage with their audience on messaging apps efficiently.

Integrating ManyChat with Zapier automates workflows between ManyChat and other apps, enabling seamless data transfer and actions based on chat interactions, further enhancing customer service efficiency.

4.8 ANALYZING YOUR COMPETITORS WITH AI TOOLS

In today's competitive digital landscape, leveraging AI tools for competitive analysis is crucial for businesses aiming to stay ahead. These tools can uncover insights into competitors' strategies, benchmark performance, identify market gaps, and adapt strategies to maintain a competitive edge.

Competitive Analysis with AI

AI tools like Smartwriter and Cohesive enable businesses to conduct comprehensive competitive analyses by identifying patterns in competitors' content and strategies. Smartwriter focuses on analyzing competitors' content to craft personalized outreach emails, integrating with email marketing tools such as Mailchimp and Sendinblue. Cohesive offers a blend of productivity and creativity, analyzing competitors' content for trends and using insights for content creation.

Benchmarking Your Performance

Tools like Semrush and Kompyte offer robust features for benchmarking marketing efforts. Semrush provides detailed analytics on competitors' traffic sources, organic search rankings, and social media performance, helping businesses understand where they stand in comparison. Kompyte tracks real-time competitor updates and offers side-by-side website comparisons, aiding in benchmarking and strategy adaptation.

Identifying Market Gaps

Exploding Topics, a trend-tracking and social listening tool, is invaluable for identifying market gaps. It analyzes social media and other channels for trending topics and emerging competitors, offering forecasts and related trends that could reveal untapped market opportunities.

Adapting Strategies Based on AI Insights

To adapt strategies effectively, it's crucial to incorporate insights derived from AI analysis into your marketing approaches. Tools like Crayon use AI to provide a comprehensive overview of competitors' pricing, products, and strategies, assisting businesses in identifying areas for improvement and differentiation.

AI Tools for Competitive Analysis

- **Smartwriter**: Specializes in creating personalized outreach strategies based on competitor analysis.
- **Cohesive**: Blends AI productivity with human creativity for content creation, including a unique text-to-image generator.
- **Semrush**: Offers extensive SEO, PPC, and social media analytics for deep competitor insights.
- **Kompyte**: Delivers real-time competitor updates and AI-driven analytics for strategic adaptation.
- **Exploding Topics**: Identifies trending topics and emerging competitors, aiding in market gap analysis.

Incorporating these AI tools into your competitive analysis strategy can transform how you understand your market position, identify opportunities, and refine your marketing efforts to outperform competitors. Whether through benchmarking performance, uncovering market gaps, or crafting data-driven marketing strategies, AI provides an indispensable competitive advantage in today's fast-paced digital world.

1. **Smartwriter**: Offers features for crafting personalized outreach emails and integrates with email marketing tools. ClickUp on Smartwriter

2. **Cohesive**: Analyzes trends in competitors' content and offers a text-to-image generator. ClickUp on Cohesive
3. **Semrush**: Provides comprehensive analytics on competitors' online presence and marketing strategies. Semrush
4. **Kompyte**: Delivers real-time competitor updates and AI-driven analytics for strategic insights. ClickUp on Kompyte
5. **Exploding Topics**: Tracks trending topics and social listening for identifying market opportunities. Exploding Topics

These tools offer various functionalities for conducting in-depth competitive analysis, benchmarking performance, identifying market gaps, and adapting strategies based on AI-driven insights.

4.9 OPTIMIZING YOUR WEBSITE WITH AI

Optimizing your website with AI involves a multi-faceted approach, focusing on improving site speed, accessibility, SEO, and content creation. AI can significantly enhance website performance by automating and optimizing various tasks:

- **Website Speed**: AI algorithms can automatically compress images and streamline website code, which can significantly lower the time it takes for pages to load. This improvement could enhance both the user experience and SEO rankings.
- **Site Accessibility**: AI can help make your site more accessible by automatically generating alt texts for images, aiding in navigation for users with disabilities, and ensuring your website meets accessibility standards.
- **Search Engine Optimization (SEO)**: AI-powered tools have the capability to analyze natural language and enhance content to improve its ranking on search engine results pages (SERPs). This helps in optimizing your website, making it appear higher in search results.They can identify keyword opportunities, suggest content ideas, and even monitor backlink profiles.
- **Content Creation**: AI-powered tools can automate aspects of content marketing, including generating blog posts, product

descriptions, and social media captions. They use natural language generation technology to create human-like text, which can improve over time with machine learning models.

Several AI SEO tools are available to help you optimize your website, including:

- **HubSpot AI Tools**: Offers SEO suggestions and content assistant tools for creating optimized blog posts, landing pages, and more.
- **SEO.ai**: Provides tools for speeding up content creation and optimization, including keyword research and AI-based suggestions.
- **GrowthBar**: An AI SEO tool that includes a built-in blog ideas generator, content writer, and meta description generator.
- **NEURONwriter**: Offers an integrated text editor, document manager, and AI templates to generate content ideas and improve collaboration efficiency.
- **Outranking**: Known for its on-page optimization features, including title, content, and internal linking analysis.

By leveraging these AI tools and strategies, you can discover untapped ranking opportunities, create and optimize content more effectively, and ultimately enhance your website's performance and user experience. Remember, the key to successful SEO in the AI era is finding unique opportunities your competition has yet to exploit, creating quality content that meets user intent, and optimizing for traditional and voice searches.

CHAPTER 5
DESIGN YOUR DESTINY WITH AI

5.1 THE INTERSECTION OF AI AND ART: AN EMERGING FRONTIER

The fusion of Artificial Intelligence (AI) and art marks a thrilling advancement in creative expression, pushing the boundaries of what's possible and redefining the essence of creativity. This section delves into how AI seamlessly integrates into the art world, transforms conventional artistic processes, and raises profound ethical questions.

Redefining Creativity

AI challenges traditional views of creativity by enabling novel forms of artistic expression. Through collaboration with AI, artists are discovering unique ways to blend technology with human ingenuity, resulting in groundbreaking works that redefine the bounds of creativity.

AI in Visual Arts

- **Dynamic Creation**: AI applications in painting, drawing, and sculpture are producing dynamic artworks that interact with viewers and change over time, offering new dimensions of engagement.

- **Interactive Experiences**: AI-driven art often involves viewer participation, where the artwork evolves based on audience interaction, making each experience unique.

The Role of AI in Modern Art

- **Exhibitions and Collaborations**: The art world is increasingly embracing AI, with exhibitions dedicated to AI art and collaborations between human artists and AI showcasing the potential of this synergy.
- **Recognition and Acceptance**: AI-created art is gaining recognition, with artworks being auctioned at prestigious venues and featured in renowned galleries, signaling a shift in the perception of AI's role in art.

Ethical Considerations

- **Authorship and Originality**: The use of AI in art raises questions about authorship and the originality of AI-generated works, challenging traditional notions of artistic creation.
- **Impact on Traditional Art**: There's an ongoing debate about the implications of AI for conventional art forms and whether AI-enhanced art could overshadow traditional techniques.

As AI continues to evolve, its integration into the art world will likely deepen, offering new avenues for creative expression while prompting important discussions on ethics, authorship, and the future of art.

AI Tools in Art

AI technologies are increasingly playing a pivotal role in art, marking a transformative era where digital innovation meets creative expression. Here's an overview of five key AI applications revolutionizing the arts:

1. Generative Adversarial Networks (GANs): These AI models have the ability to produce images that are astonishingly lifelike, pushing the boundaries of what's considered possible in art and creativity.
2. AI in Music Creation: With AI algorithms at their core, these tools are capable of crafting musical pieces and merging various styles and genres into unique compositions.
3. AI-Powered Interactive Art: These installations adapt and evolve based on viewer interaction, offering personalized and engaging immersive experiences.
4. AI for Writing and Poetry: This software leverages AI to craft poetry, narratives, and even screenplays, opening new avenues for storytelling and literary invention.
5. AI in Video and Animation Creation: These tools enable the production of animated content or videos, simplifying the process of generating visually compelling media with fewer human resources.

The fusion of AI with artistic endeavors signifies more than just technological progress; it represents a novel paradigm in understanding creativity and expression. As AI technology advances, its capacity to redefine the art landscape grows, signaling a future where innovation and human creativity interlace more seamlessly than ever.

Exploring the dynamic intersection of AI and art, I found several innovative tools that epitomize this fusion, offering a broad range of creative possibilities:

1. **DALL·E 3 by OpenAI**: An advanced iteration of the DALL·E series, DALL·E 3 is capable of producing intricate and personalized images based on text inputs. Its integration with ChatGPT Plus enhances the user's control over the creative process, making it a top choice for those looking for ease of use and quality results.
2. **DreamStudio by Stable Diffusion**: Known for its customization capabilities, DreamStudio allows users to fine-tune the AI's operations, such as adjusting the number of steps taken or the random seed used. It offers a trial with

free credits, appealing to users wanting a balance of power and affordability.

3. **Midjourney**: Unique for its interface through Discord, Midjourney produces some of the most visually impressive and realistic results among AI art generators. It's particularly favored for its quality outcomes despite its unconventional access method.

4. **Canva's AI Art Generator**: Canva has integrated an AI text-to-image generator, merging seamlessly with its extensive design toolset. This addition makes it effortless to incorporate AI-generated art into various designs, from social media posts to greeting cards, offering a practical solution for designers seeking to enhance their creations.

5. **NightCafe**: This platform supports many AI art models and stands out for its community features, such as challenges and a Discord server. It's designed for enthusiasts of AI art, providing tools for both creation and interaction with a like-minded community.

6. **OpenArt**: OpenArt enhances popular models like Stable Diffusion and DALL·E 2 with additional features and greater control over image generation. It's also noteworthy for its free trial and sketch-to-image feature, appealing to those seeking versatility and customization.

7. **Adobe Firefly**: Adobe's entry into AI-generated art, Firefly, is noted for its integration within Adobe products and its unique ability to create custom text effects. This tool caters to users seeking a professional-grade solution that blends with existing workflows.

8. **Jasper Art**: Originally known for AI writing tools, Jasper also offers an art generator capable of producing unlimited images for a monthly fee. It's suited for users already utilizing Jasper for content creation and looking to expand into visual art.

9. **Hypotenuse:** Offers a variety of drawing styles and is easy to use. Plans start at $24/month for 200 watermark-free AI images. However, it doesn't support widescreen, high-resolution images.

10. **Lensa AI by Prisma Labs:** Is popular for its "Magic Avatars" feature, which generates AI-powered selfies from uploaded photos. This app provides a range of AI-powered image editing features.
11. **Stablecog:** A new, free AI image generator that allows users to create various styles of AI art. It's notable for its no-sign-up, unlimited free use policy, support for multiple languages, and custom models.

These AI-powered tools cater to diverse needs, from professional design work to personal art projects.

5.2 AI TOOLS FOR GRAPHIC DESIGN: UNLEASHING CREATIVITY

Integrating Artificial Intelligence in graphic design is revolutionizing how we create and interact with visual content. AI technology helps designers by giving them powerful tools to easily create impressive visuals, making the design process more efficient.

These tools illustrate AI's vast potential to transform graphic design, making advanced editing techniques more accessible and opening up new creative possibilities for designers. As AI continues to evolve, we can expect even more innovative applications that blur the lines between technology and art, empowering designers to unleash their full creative potential.

- **Automating Design Tasks**: AI tools significantly reduce the time spent on repetitive tasks. By automating these tasks, designers are liberated to invest their efforts in the more creative aspects of their projects.
- **Enhancing Visual Content**: Advanced AI algorithms can dramatically improve the quality of photos and videos. Techniques like upscaling resolution and correcting imperfections ensure visual content reaches a higher standard of excellence.
- **AI-Powered Design Platforms**: Several platforms leverage AI to assist designers in creating sophisticated designs,

logos, and branding materials efficiently. These platforms require minimal input, making them accessible to both seasoned designers and those with less experience.

- **Collaboration Between AI and Designers**: The most innovative designs often come from a partnership between AI and human creativity. This collaboration highlights the potential for AI to augment human skills, leading to groundbreaking and inventive outcomes.

AI Tools for Graphic Design: Examples

Among the top AI tools transforming the industry, **Uizard** stands out by digitizing hand-drawn sketches into digital design files, facilitating the prototyping process. **Adobe Firefly**, part of Adobe's suite, uses AI to create and edit images, enhancing creative processes with ease. **Midjourney** utilizes AI to transform text prompts into realistic images, making it a powerful tool for visual content creation. Known for its user-friendly interface, Canva incorporates AI features to streamline design tasks, offering a vast library of templates and design elements. **Khroma** uses AI to generate color palettes based on user preferences, aiding designers in maintaining color consistency across their projects.

Other notable tools include **Designify,** which uses AI to automatically enhance and transform photos, and **Let's Enhance,** an AI tool that increases image resolution without losing detail, ideal for printing and large displays. Deep Dream Generator utilizes AI to create surreal and unique images by applying deep neural network-based artistic effects, while **Autodraw** helps users create polished drawings quickly by suggesting professional-looking alternatives to hand-drawn sketches. **Pikazo** and **Prisma** are AI apps that transform photos into artworks by applying various artistic styles, enhancing creativity and expression in digital art.

For background removal, **Remove.bg** specializes in precision editing tasks with just a click, while **DeepArt.io** and **Artisto** transform photos and videos into digital artworks using AI. **ColorMind** is an AI-powered color scheme generator that creates harmonious color palettes, aiding designers in choosing the perfect colors for their projects. **Runway ML** provides AI tools for creating and editing images and videos, including automated background removal and style transfer. **Stencil** and **Snappa** streamline the creation of social media graphics with their easy-to-use interfaces and wide arrays of templates, while **Easil** and **RelayThat** offer drag-and-drop simplicity with vast libraries of templates and design elements, helping create consistent and branded marketing materials.

5.3 WRITING WITH AI: FROM NOVELS TO SCRIPTS

The landscape of writing, ranging from novels to scripts and beyond, has been significantly transformed by the advent of Artificial Intelligence. AI's role in assisting writers, enhancing creativity in storytelling, reshaping journalism, and navigating AI's ethical and creative implications in writing is vast and nuanced.

AI-Assisted Writing

AI writing tools offer a range of functionalities designed to assist in the writing process. These tools can generate ideas, create outlines, and suggest style and grammar improvements. Platforms like **Writesonic**, **Sudowrite**, and **GrowthBar** exemplify the diversity and power of AI in automating and enhancing the writing process.

Creative Storytelling with AI

AI's capacity to contribute to plot development and character creation is groundbreaking in creative storytelling. Tools like **ClickUp AI** and **Rytr** leverage AI's capabilities to beat writer's block and streamline content creation across various formats, including narratives, novels, scripts, and poetry.

AI in Journalism

Journalism has also seen a profound impact from AI, with tools facilitating automated news reporting and data journalism. This innovation heralds a new era for the field, where the speed and accuracy of information dissemination are significantly improved. **ClickUp AI**, for example, demonstrates the utility of AI in generating content outlines and high-quality marketing copy that can be used in journalistic contexts.

Ethical and Creative Implications

The use of AI in writing raises important questions about authenticity, copyright, and the evolving role of human writers. As AI tools become more prevalent, the lines between human creativity and machine-generated content blur, prompting a reevaluation of the creative process and intellectual property rights.

AI Tools for Writing: Examples

Several AI tools have made significant strides in transforming the writing landscape:

1. **Writesonic**: Ideal for generating high-quality content, offering features like spell checking, grammar correction, and customizable templates.
2. **Sudowrite**: A user-friendly tool for enhancing productivity and ensuring accuracy in content production.
3. **GrowthBar**: Provides ideas, generates outlines, and offers SEO recommendations to optimize content.
4. **QuillBot**: Known for its paraphrasing capabilities, helping writers rephrase and enhance their content with ease.
5. **Frase.io**: This tool aids in generating content, improving writing, and optimizing SEO, making it particularly useful for SEO teams and content managers.

An additional 30+ writing AI tools are available to access at this link: https://aiwealthentrepreneur.com/tools

5.4 MUSIC COMPOSITION WITH AI: A NEW ERA FOR MUSICIANS

Integrating Artificial Intelligence (AI) in music composition has inaugurated a new chapter for musicians, enabling a fusion of human creativity with computational ingenuity. This synergy not only expands the horizons of musical creativity but also introduces efficiency and innovation in music production.

AI-Generated Music

AI systems have been developed to compose music across various genres, offering tools that inspire musicians to explore new compositions. These AI music generators, like **Soundraw**, **Artlist**, and **AIVA**, provide platforms where music can be created with minimal input, producing complex and engaging outputs. **Soundraw**, for instance, is celebrated for its generative music capabilities that craft original music based on user preferences, making it a preferred choice for those seeking control over their musical outputs.

Collaboration Between AI and Musicians

The collaboration between AI and musicians is not just theoretical but a practical reality, evidenced by various case studies. Musicians use AI as a collaborative partner, blending human emotion and AI's computational abilities to produce unique compositions. Tools like **Amper Music** and **MuseNet** are notable for their ability to generate music for various applications, from podcasts to video games, serving as a testament to the creative partnerships between AI and artists.

The Future of Music Production

AI is revolutionizing music production by automating aspects like mixing, mastering, and creating virtual instruments and sounds. AI music generators like **Ecrett Music** and **Melody Scanner** offer innovative approaches to music creation, allowing for customization and easy music generation. These advancements hint at a future where music production is more accessible and enriched with endless possibilities.

Challenges and Opportunities

Despite the exciting prospects, integrating AI into the music creation process presents challenges. Musicians grapple with maintaining artistic integrity while navigating the technology's limitations. However, the opportunities for creativity and innovation are immense. Platforms like **BandLab SongStarter** and **Google Tone Transfer** illustrate how AI can serve both beginners and seasoned musicians by offering inspiration and novel tools for music production.

AI Tools for Music Composition: Examples

- **MuseNet** - OpenAI's deep neural network trained to generate music.
- **Endlesss** - A collaborative music creation platform.
- **AIVA** - An AI that composes classical music.
- **Amper Music** - An AI-driven music composition tool.
- **Humtap** - AI that turns your humming into music.

- **Beatoven.ai** - AI-generated royalty-free music for content creators.
- **Ecrett Music** - A user-friendly music generator for video creators.
- **Alyx** - An AI music generator for creating soundtracks.
- **Lander** - An AI mastering tool for audio tracks.
- **Jukedeck** - AI-powered music composition for content creators.

Each tool provides distinct features and benefits, from MuseNet's advanced generative capabilities to **Soundraw**'s deep learning technology for quickly and easily creating music pieces. **AIVA**'s deep learning algorithms analyze vast amounts of musical data to generate unique compositions, making it an excellent choice for professionals.

These AI music generators illustrate the transformative impact of technology on music creation, offering both challenges and opportunities for musicians and creators. The blend of AI and music composition marks the beginning of a new era in the creative landscape, continually evolving as technology advances.

Integrating AI in music composition marks the beginning of a transformative era for musicians, presenting a blend of challenges and opportunities. As technology continues to progress, it will inevitably impact the manner in which we produce, participate in, and communicate through music.

5.5 AI IN PHOTOGRAPHY AND VIDEOGRAPHY: ENHANCING VISUALS

Integrating Artificial Intelligence (AI) in photography and videography is revolutionizing how we create and interact with visual media. AI technology helps make pictures and videos better and more interesting. It's like a tool that artists and creators can use to make their work faster and better. It can help them develop new ideas and make their work more exciting.

Automated Photo Editing

AI photo editing tools automate and streamline various tasks that traditionally require extensive manual effort. Software like Adobe

Photoshop and Luminar Neo provide AI-driven features for enhancing image quality, removing objects, and applying stylized edits with precision and ease. Aftershoot, for example, automates the culling process in photography, learning from your previous edits to make smarter selections, while Adobe Photoshop leverages AI for object selection and content-aware fill, among other features.

AI in Video Production

In video production, AI is making significant strides in automating editing, generating visual effects, and creating animations. These tools enable creators to produce high-quality videos faster and more efficiently. AI technologies in video editing software help streamline the production process, from initial editing to final touches, allowing for more creativity and experimentation.

AI for Enhanced Creativity in Visual Media

AI opens up new ways for creativity in visual media, enabling photographers and videographers to achieve effects and visuals that were previously impossible or highly time-consuming. Tools like DeepArt.io transform photos into artworks using different stylistic effects applied through AI, illustrating the potential of AI to enhance creative expression.

Ethical Considerations in Visual Media

The use of AI in photography and videography raises important ethical considerations regarding authenticity, manipulation, and privacy. While AI can significantly enhance the creative process, creators must navigate these technologies responsibly, ensuring that their use of AI upholds the integrity of their work and respects individuals' privacy.

AI Tools for Photography and Videography: Examples

- **Adobe Photoshop**: A staple in photo editing, now incorporating AI tools for object selection and style transfer.
- **Luminar Neo**: Known for its AI-driven editing capabilities, offering a range of automated enhancements and effects.
- **Remove.bg**: Specializes in removing backgrounds from photos with just a click, demonstrating AI's precision in editing tasks.

- **DeepArt.io**: Allows users to turn their photos into digital artworks by applying various artistic styles through AI.
- **Topaz Labs**: Offers a suite of AI tools, including DeNoise AI for noise reduction and Sharpen AI for image sharpening.

These tools illustrate just a fraction of AI's potential to transform photography and videography, making advanced editing techniques more accessible and opening up new creative possibilities for visual artists. As AI continues to evolve, we'll likely see even more innovative applications that blur the lines between technology and art.

5.6 AI AND GAME DEVELOPMENT: CREATING NEW WORLDS

The fusion of Artificial Intelligence (AI) with game development is pioneering new frontiers, transforming how games are designed, developed, and experienced. This evolution is not just about enhancing game visuals or mechanics but redefining the entire gaming landscape.

Procedural Content Generation

Procedural Content Generation stands at the forefront of AI's integration into game development, offering a paradigm shift in how game environments, levels, and assets are created. AI algorithms are employed to generate vast and diverse game worlds, providing gamers with endless variety and replayability. Tools like Scenario and Promethean AI exemplify this trend, enabling developers to create high-quality game art and 3D environments that are both unique and aligned with specific artistic visions or environmental requirements.

AI for Dynamic Gameplay

Dynamic gameplay, powered by AI, adapts to the player's actions, ensuring a deeply immersive and personalized gaming experience. Ludo.ai is an example of how AI can analyze player behavior and adapt gameplay accordingly, offering tailored experiences that enhance player engagement and satisfaction.

The Role of AI in Narrative Design

AI's role extends into narrative design, where it is used to create complex storylines and character interactions that respond dynamically to player choices. Charisma, for example, leverages AI to generate immersive narratives, providing a new level of depth and interactivity in game stories, with storylines and dialogues that can adapt based on the player's decisions.

Challenges in Integrating AI into Games

While AI offers vast potential for game development, integrating it into games comes with its set of challenges, both technical and creative. However, platforms like Unity are overcoming these hurdles by providing developers with AI-driven tools like Unity Muse and Unity Sentis, which enhance real-time 3D experiences and enable AI models in the Unity Runtime.

Moreover, AI assists in areas like playtesting, cheat detection, content moderation, and even acting as player stand-ins through bots, demonstrating its versatility and indispensability in modern game development. The use of AI bots for playtesting, for instance, allows for quick, constant, and systematic testing that can significantly speed up the development process.

AI Tools for Game Development: Examples

1. **Scenario**: Specializes in AI-powered game art creation, offering fine-tuning capabilities to align with specific art directions.
2. **Promethean AI**: Automates the building of 3D environments, facilitating the creation of detailed game worlds.
3. **Unity Muse & Unity Sentis**: Offer game and real-time 3D experience development tools powered by AI to enhance creative and operational efficiencies.
4. **Charisma**: Enables the generation of dynamic narratives and characters, enriching game storytelling.
5. **modl.ai**: Provides AI-driven tools for building better games, accelerating the game development process, and enhancing player engagement.

The use of AI in game development is constantly evolving, providing game developers and players with exciting new opportunities for creativity, immersion, and interaction. This integration of AI into gaming offers a whole new world of possibilities that everyone can explore.

5.7 MONETIZING AI ART: PLATFORMS AND STRATEGIES

The advent of AI in the art world has opened up innovative avenues for artists to create and monetize their artworks. AI-generated art can be sold and promoted through various platforms, each offering unique opportunities to reach wider audiences and generate income.

Below are strategies and platforms to help AI artists thrive in the digital age.

Selling AI-Created Artworks

Leveraging digital marketplaces and NFT platforms is a promising strategy to monetize AI-created artworks. Platforms like eBay, Alamy, and Society6 offer artists opportunities to showcase and sell their AI artworks to a global audience. eBay, for example, allows listing AI art items for auction or at fixed prices, while Alamy pays up to 50% of sales made through its website. Additionally, Wirestock serves as a centralized platform, offering artists access to the world's leading marketplaces like Adobe Stock and Dreamstime, streamlining the selling process.

Licensing AI-Generated Content

Licensing offers another lucrative avenue, especially for AI-generated content ranging from stock photos to music compositions. Platforms like BigStockPhoto and Dreamstime facilitate the sale and licensing of AI-generated images, vectors, and illustrations, with artists earning a commission for every artwork sold.

Crowdfunding and Patronage

Crowdfunding and patronage platforms like Patreon enable artists to fund AI art projects while building a supportive community. By engaging with their audience, artists can receive financial support directly from fans and patrons who value their work.

Building a Brand Around AI Art

Creating a personal or business brand around AI art involves effective marketing strategies and community engagement. Artists can use social media platforms to showcase their AI artworks, connect with like-minded individuals, and engage with a broader audience. Wirestock also offers a unique opportunity for artists to join a vibrant community of AI art enthusiasts, fostering collaboration and idea exchange.

Turning AI art into Non-Fungible Tokens (NFTs) offers another lucrative channel for monetization, allowing artists to tokenize their digital creations on blockchain platforms. This secures the artwork's authenticity and ownership and enables artists to earn through resale royalties. Platforms like OpenSea, Rarible, and Foundation facilitate the minting and trading of NFTs, providing artists with a global marketplace to sell their unique AI-generated art pieces. This process empowers creators to capitalize on the growing interest in digital and crypto art, further expanding the avenues for monetizing AI art in the digital age.

AI Tools and Platforms for Monetizing Art

- **Wirestock**: A comprehensive AI art marketplace that simplifies the process of selling AI-generated artwork across multiple platforms.
- **eBay and Alamy** Offer platforms for artists to list and sell their AI artworks. eBay supports auction and fixed-price formats, and Alamy provides a high commission rate for sales.
- **BigStockPhoto and Dreamstime**: Ideal for selling high-quality AI-generated images and illustrations, offering competitive commission rates and broad exposure.
- **Society6**: A platform that not only allows selling AI art but also enables artists to feature their works on a variety of products, thus increasing their visibility and potential income.

In conclusion, monetizing AI art involves exploring various platforms and strategies tailored to AI artists' unique capabilities and interests. Social media channels, particularly Instagram and TikTok, can be used to build a following and attract potential buyers through engaging content and storytelling. Moreover, collaborations with brands and businesses for custom AI-generated designs can provide lucrative opportunities. AI artists can monetize their creations and thrive in the digital age by employing these strategies and using the right platforms. From selling and licensing artworks to crowdfunding and brand building, artists have numerous opportunities to capitalize on their creations. Leveraging these platforms and strategies effectively can help artists navigate the evolving landscape of AI art and achieve success.

5.8 SUCCESS STORIES: REAL EXAMPLES OF AI PASSIVE INCOME

Case Study 1: AI-Driven Content Creation - Lil Miquela

Lil Miquela, crafted by the Los Angeles-based startup Brud, valued at $125 million, is a prime example of AI-driven content creation. Since 2016, this virtual influencer has amassed a significant following, with an estimated net worth of $10 million by August 2023. Her success on platforms like Instagram, where she charges up to $10,000 per post, underscores the potential of AI in generating passive income through digital influence and content creation. Miquela's collaborations with major brands, including Samsung and Prada, highlight her impact on virtual influencer marketing.

How To Create a Realistic AI Influencer

Creating a realistic AI influencer and monetizing it involves several steps, from generating AI influencer images to marketing and optimizing your content for social media platforms like Instagram and TikTok. Here's a condensed overview based on the information gathered:

1. **Setting Up the AI Influencer**: Initially, you'll need to install the necessary programs and tools for creating AI-generated images. This includes using AI face swap web UIs and extensions like Roof to enhance the capabilities of your generator.
2. **Generating AI Influencer Images**: Tools like Mid-Journey can generate AI influencer images. You'll need to gather reference images, describe these images to Mid-Journey, and

then upload these reference images to Mid-Journey's Discord to refine the generated images.

3. **Creating a Social Media Presence**: Once you have your AI influencer images, the next step is to create a social media account for your influencer. This involves crafting a unique influencer persona, sharing AI-generated content, and engaging with your audience.

4. **Monetization Strategies**: To make money from your AI influencer, it's essential to determine the best times to post, use effective hashtags, and explore different sources of income, such as affiliate marketing, selling products, advertising revenue, partnerships, and platforms like OnlyFans.

This approach offers a creative outlet for generating unique digital content and opens up new possibilities for branding and marketing in the digital age. By following these steps and considering the ethical implications of AI-generated content, you can successfully create and monetize an AI influencer.

Case Study 2: E-commerce Automation

In the e-commerce sector, AI has revolutionized how businesses operate and scale. For example, companies like Netflix and Spotify utilize AI to analyze user data for personalized content recommendations. This approach enhances user experience and streamlines operations, leading to increased sales and customer retention. By leveraging AI for product recommendations and inventory management tasks, e-commerce businesses can achieve significant growth and generate passive income through efficient and personalized customer engagement.

Dictador, a renowned Polish luxury rum producer, took a groundbreaking step by appointing an AI humanoid robot named Mika as its CEO. This marked a significant leap in integrating technology with traditional business practices, as Mika became the world's first AI CEO in the industry. Operating non-stop, Mika's key responsibilities include scouting for potential clients and leading the creative process for rum bottle labels, blending creativity with AI precision. Under her leadership, Dictador enhanced its business processes and set a precedent for future corporate management, showcasing the potential of AI in leadership roles.

Case Study 3: AI in Affiliate Marketing

The range of earnings generated through AI affiliate marketing varies widely. It is affected by factors such as the affiliate's level of expertise, the niche they choose to focus on, and how they strategically implement affiliate programs. This case study synthesizes insights from ClickBank, Diggity Marketing, and Influencer Marketing Hub to highlight the variability in earnings and factors contributing to success in affiliate marketing.

Experience and Earnings: Earnings vary significantly by experience level. Beginners typically earn between $0 to $1,000 per month, intermediates see $1,000 to $10,000, advanced affiliates can make $10k to $100k, and super affiliates often exceed $100k per month.

Incorporating AI in affiliate marketing through platforms like ClickBank revolutionizes the approach by enabling highly targeted and personalized outreach, optimizing campaign performances in real-time, aiding in creating SEO-optimized content, and utilizing predictive analytics to foresee trends and consumer behaviors, thereby maximizing the potential for success.

The use of AI in affiliate marketing demonstrates how technology can enhance the personalization and efficiency of marketing efforts, leading to better outcomes for both marketers and consumers.

By embracing AI, individuals and businesses can unlock new opportunities for growth and passive income generation in the digital age.

Case Study 4: AI-Generated Music

A compelling case study about making money with AI-generated music involves the platform Mubert and its users, both content creators and contributing artists. Mubert's platform allows users to generate AI music tracks to accompany various forms of content, such as videos on YouTube and social media. This ecosystem supports the rapidly growing Creator Economy, providing legal music to accompany content. Interestingly, only a tiny fraction of creators (5%) have reported AI-supported content as a significant source of income, with another 3% earning a moderate amount. Most are either in the early stages of monetization or have yet to earn money from AI-generated content. However, Mubert also supports artists by compensating them for contributing audio samples to train its algorithms, with one of the most active contributors earning $14,836 from submitting nearly 27,000 pieces.

Another intriguing aspect is the emergence of AI-generated songs on streaming platforms like Spotify, which has sparked curiosity and legal concerns. A notable example involves a Spotify user who discovered multiple songs with near-identical audio but different titles and artists, compiled into a playlist of 49 tracks. This highlighted the peculiar phenomenon of AI-generated music infiltrating streaming services. The situation raised questions about the responsibility of platforms in hosting AI-generated content, copyright infringement, and the impact on artistic integrity. Additionally, the case of an AI-generated song resembling the styles of Drake and The Weeknd, "Heart on My Sleeve," stirred debate over copyright, rights of publicity, and the legal complexities of AI-generated music. This case underscores the legal and ethical challenges that arise as AI-generated music becomes more prevalent in the industry.

Generating income can be done in various ways, such as producing AI-generated music and utilizing it across different platforms while also having a good grasp of the legal implications involved.

Case Study 4: AI-Generated Photography and Art

The digital camera industry, as of 2021, was valued at $8.2 billion and is expected to see significant growth, reaching a market value growth of $12.1 billion by 2028. This indicates a growing interest and investment in photography technology, which includes AI advancements.

"Crossroads" by Beeple is a remarkable AI-generated piece that vividly combines surreal and dystopian elements. This artwork, selling as an NFT for $6.6 million, not only highlights the financial potential of digital and AI-generated art but also emphasizes the evolving narrative capabilities of AI in creating complex visual stories. The artwork of Beeple is a remarkable illustration of how artificial intelligence is expanding the limits of creativity and the assessment of art in the modern era.

In a riveting blend of artificial intelligence and artistry, Damien Hirst's "The Beautiful Paintings" project, employing AI to allow collectors to create customized artworks, astonishingly amassed $20 million in sales over nine days. This endeavor highlights Hirst's innovative merge of technology with his iconic spin painting technique. It underscores the shifting paradigms of art collection and the enduring allure of physical artworks over their digital counterparts, marking a significant moment in the evolution of art consumption and investment.

By employing AI tools for tasks like content creation and online advertising, individuals can streamline their workflows and open new channels for passive income. These AI technologies enhance productivity and enable entrepreneurs to explore novel business opportunities with minimal effort.

As the boundary between reality and AI becomes increasingly indistinct, we're witnessing the potential transformation of influencer and social media marketing. The next billion-dollar consumer brand could emerge from AI-generated social media models, indicating a significant shift in how companies approach marketing and brand building. This evolution reflects a broader trend where AI's role in creative and executive capacities is not just a possibility but an imminent reality, reshaping industries and redefining the future of work and marketing.

In conclusion, anyone can make money online with artificial intelligence in just 30 minutes a day if you master AI tools and follow the guidelines outlined in this book. The advancements in AI technology have democratized access to powerful resources that can automate tasks, optimize strategies, and generate income streams with minimal time investment. By leveraging the tools and techniques discussed, you can effectively harness AI to create and grow your online business. Whether you are new to the field or an experienced entrepreneur, dedicating a small portion of your day to implementing these strategies can lead to significant financial gains. Remember, consistency and dedication to mastering these tools are key to unlocking the full potential of AI in your online ventures.

FREE BONUS "100+ AI Tools"

Unlock the full potential of your creative projects with our exclusive "100+ AI Tools" spreadsheet, available as a **free bonus**!

Whether you're into music, photography, video games and writing, this comprehensive resource has got you covered. Click on the link **below https://aiwealthentrepreneur.com/tools or scan the QR code:**

to access it now and explore the latest AI 100+ tools to elevate your work, streamline your processes, and inspire new ideas. Don't miss out on this essential guide – your ultimate AI toolkit is just a click away!

TITLE: MAKE A DIFFERENCE WITH YOUR REVIEW

Unlock the Power of Earning Online

> "HELPING OTHERS ACHIEVE THEIR DREAMS
> AND FINDING YOUR OWN HAPPINESS ALONG
> THE WAY, THAT'S THE TRUE ESSENCE OF
> SUCCESS." -MONIKA ALI KHAN

If we can spread joy and prosperity while navigating through life's pages, why wouldn't we? I've got a small request that can make a big impact...

Would you like to be a guiding star for someone you've never met, expecting nothing in return?

Think about who this person might be: someone like you were before reading this book. They're eager to change their world, curious about making money online with AI, and just need a little guidance.

Our mission is to demystify the secrets of online wealth for everyone. Every word in this book is written with that goal in mind. But to make a real difference, we need to reach as many people as possible.

This is where you come in. People do judge a book by its cover—and by what others say about it. So, on behalf of a future entrepreneur, I'm asking:

Could you take a moment to leave a review for this book?

It costs nothing and takes only a minute, but it could change another dreamer's life. Your words might help:

- One more startup to flourish.
- One more visionary to support their loved ones.
- One more individual to find their calling.
- One more transformation to begin.
- One more dream to be realized.

To make a difference and feel that warm glow, it takes less than a magic minute to leave a review. Just scan the QR code below and share your thoughts:

https://www.amazon.com/review/review-your-purchases/?asin=191734001X

If the thought of anonymously uplifting another soul warms your heart, then you are indeed a rare gem. Welcome aboard our tribe.

I'm excited to help you unlock the secrets of online wealth more easily than ever. You're going to love the strategies and insights in the upcoming chapters.

With deep gratitude,

Monika

P.S. Adding value to someone's life increases your value in their eyes. If you believe this book can guide someone to prosperity, why not share it with them?

CHAPTER 6
BROADENING YOUR AI INCOME STREAMS

6.1 AI IN REAL ESTATE: STREAMLINING OPERATIONS AND SALES

The integration of Artificial Intelligence (AI) in real estate is revolutionizing the industry, offering new ways to streamline operations and enhance sales efforts. Here's how AI is making an impact:

- **Predictive Analytics for Property Valuation**: AI tools like Zillow Zestimate and HouseCanary utilize vast datasets and machine learning algorithms to provide precise property valuations and market trends analysis. Using this innovative technology, real estate professionals can provide clients with data-supported advice. This approach ensures that clients can make informed decisions and receive competitive pricing.

- **Automating Property Management Tasks**: CRM platforms such as Zoho CRM and Real Geeks offer AI-enhanced functionalities to automate client management and sales processes. These tools help organize client information, track and nurture leads, and develop targeted marketing strategies, ultimately improving client engagement and sales outcomes.

- **Virtual Property Tours**: Platforms like Matterport and Virtual Staging AI are at the forefront of virtual staging and tours, creating immersive and interactive experiences for potential buyers. These AI tools enable real estate agents to present properties dynamically, appealing to a broader audience and reducing the need for physical showings.
- **AI in Real Estate Investment**: Investment platforms such as Entera leverage AI to automate and provide intelligent analytics for property investments. By analyzing market data, these platforms help investors identify lucrative opportunities, manage assets, and optimize their investment portfolios for maximum returns.

Platforms and Tools Overview

- **Marketing and Content Creation**: Tools like Saleswise and listingcopy.ai are revolutionizing real estate marketing by generating AI-driven marketing copy, emails, and scripts, enhancing the efficiency and impact of marketing strategies.
- **Customer Relationship Management**: Zoho CRM and Real Geeks offer robust CRM solutions tailored for the real estate industry. These solutions enhance lead management and client engagement through AI-powered insights and automation.
- **Property Showcasing and Staging**: Matterport and Virtual Staging AI provide innovative solutions for virtual tours and staging, enabling agents to offer captivating property presentations and reach potential buyers globally.
- **Investment Analytics**: Platforms such as Entera and HouseCanary harness the power of AI to provide cutting-edge analytics and insights for real estate investments.

Integrating AI into real estate doesn't just streamline and automate tasks; it also creates new avenues for generating income and expanding into new markets. By leveraging these tools, real estate professionals can enhance their operational efficiency, improve customer engagement, and drive sales and investment success.

6.2: EDUCATIONAL CONTENT AND AI: REVOLUTIONIZING LEARNING

The advent of Artificial Intelligence (AI) in education is transforming traditional teaching methods and learning experiences, paving the way for a future where personalized and interactive learning environments are the norm.

Personalized Learning Paths

AI facilitates personalized learning experiences by adapting to each student's learning pace and style in real time. ClickUp, as highlighted in the educational landscape of 2024, serves as an exemplary model, offering a suite of organizational and AI-driven features designed to optimize student success.

AI-Driven Content Creation

AI's role in generating educational content is revolutionizing the way materials are produced. For example, Course Hero utilizes AI to provide instant answers and detailed explanations across a wide range of study materials, demonstrating the platform's ability to leverage AI for enhanced academic learning and efficiency.

Automated Grading and Feedback

Gradescope is an innovative AI-enhanced platform that streamlines the grading process, offering detailed rubrics and batch grading for consistency and speed. This technology not only saves educators time but also provides students with clear, actionable feedback.

Monetizing AI in Education

Exploring ways to monetize AI in education reveals a rich landscape of opportunities. Similar to the strategies mentioned, such as subscription models and licensing agreements, several innovative AI tools are transforming the educational sector:

1. **Pictory** is an AI platform that converts written scripts or articles into engaging videos. It's beneficial for creating educational content that's visually captivating. The tool automates the storyboard and visual generation process, making video creation accessible to educators and content creators.

2. **Canva Classroom Magic** provides educators with AI tools to generate visual and written content seamlessly. It's incorporated into Canva, making it easier to create captivating and educational materials. This suite of tools is part of Canva's broader educational offering and is designed to support teachers in creating more dynamic learning environments.

3. **Curipod** leverages AI to produce interactive slide decks for classroom use. With features like polls, word clouds, and drawing tools, it supports an interactive learning experience. The platform generates 9-12 slides on a chosen topic, which can then be customized to fit the lesson plan.

4. **Diffit** is an AI tool that customizes reading materials to different levels and languages, generating "just right" resources for any topic. This tool helps adapt existing materials for all readers, making it easier for teachers to meet the diverse needs of their students.

5. **MagicSchool.ai** is an educational platform powered by AI that automates tasks like lesson planning and grading. It provides over 40 AI tools, searchable by keyword, to support planning, student assistance, and productivity. This platform is trained on best practices for educators and ensures compliance with educational regulations.

These examples illustrate just a few ways AI is being harnessed to enrich educational content and streamline administrative tasks, thereby opening new avenues for monetization. By offering subscription services or licensing their AI technologies, companies behind these tools can provide value-added services to educational institutions and content creators, enhancing learning experiences while generating sustainable revenue.

6.3: AI IN HEALTHCARE: OPPORTUNITIES FOR INNOVATION

AI in Diagnosis and Treatment Planning

AI's integration into healthcare is revolutionizing the way diseases are diagnosed and treated. By leveraging machine learning (ML) and natural language processing (NLP), AI algorithms are significantly improving data analysis, enabling the identification of patterns that might elude manual discovery. For instance, the Renal Research Institute employs AI and ML to diagnose and manage kidney disease, predicting patient outcomes and analyzing images for better diagnosis. Similarly, advancements in medical diagnostics are facilitated by AI, as startups develop technologies for early disease detection and the analysis of patient datasets for chronic conditions prevention.

Automating Administrative Tasks in Healthcare

Generative AI (Gen AI) is being explored for its potential to automate numerous administrative tasks in hospitals, such as generating discharge summaries, synthesizing care coordination notes, and even creating checklists in real-time. By reducing the time and money spent on administrative costs, Gen AI could significantly enhance operational efficiency and address workforce shortages.

AI-Powered Health Monitoring Devices

The market for AI-powered wearable and home monitoring devices is expanding, driven by the need for continuous health management. These devices, backed by AI algorithms, can monitor a wide range of health metrics, offering new opportunities for personalized health care and proactive disease management. The World Economic Forum highlights AI's role in making healthcare more accurate, accessible, and sustainable, underscoring the importance of AI in improving health outcomes through innovative monitoring solutions.

Leveraging AI for Health Education

AI's capability to personalize health education content is proving to be a game-changer. By analyzing vast amounts of data, AI can tailor educational materials to individual needs, enhancing understanding and engagement with health-related information. This personalization opens up avenues for monetization through health education apps and online platforms, providing users with access to customized health information and advice.

The field of AI in healthcare is vast and constantly evolving, with technologies like ML, NLP, and gen AI leading the charge in transforming clinical care, diagnostics, patient safety, and more. As these innovations continue to develop, they offer promising opportunities for enhancing patient care, streamlining healthcare operations, and creating new markets for AI-powered health solutions.

6.4: AI FOR PERSONAL FINANCE MANAGEMENT

The integration of Artificial Intelligence (AI) into personal finance is transforming the way we manage our money, offering unprecedented opportunities for both consumers and financial institutions.

AI-Driven Personal Finance Assistants

AI personal finance assistants are revolutionizing budgeting, investing, and financial planning. By analyzing spending habits and financial goals, these assistants provide tailored advice and proactive alerts to help users make informed financial decisions. However, while AI offers personalized insights, it's important to remember its limitations, such as a lack of emotional intelligence and the possibility of algorithmic bias. Balancing AI recommendations with human judgment ensures financial decisions align with personal values and goals.

Automating Investment Analysis

AI significantly enhances investment analysis by managing portfolios, analyzing market trends, and predicting future opportunities. By leveraging vast amounts of data, AI tools provide investors with insights that can lead to more informed decision-making. Generative AI, in particular, is starting to play a transformative role in finance, impacting everything from financial reporting to risk mitigation efforts .

Fraud Detection and Security

AI's ability to detect fraudulent activities and unauthorized transactions is crucial for enhancing financial security. By examining financial data in real time, AI systems identify patterns indicative of fraud, thereby protecting users' financial assets more effectively.

Monetizing Financial Planning Services

The monetization of AI-driven financial planning and advisory services presents significant opportunities. Subscription models, premium app features, and personalized consulting services are just a few avenues through which financial institutions and fintech startups can generate revenue. As AI continues to mature, its integration into personal finance apps and platforms will likely become a necessity rather than a luxury.

As AI for personal finance evolves, the focus remains on creating innovative, trustworthy, and secure tools. Addressing challenges related to data privacy, regulatory compliance, and user trust will be key to fully realizing AI's potential in personal finance. By marrying AI's analytical capabilities with human insight and understanding, we can look forward to a future where managing personal finances is more efficient, accessible, and aligned with individual financial goals.

6.5: AI IN AGRICULTURE: FARMING OF THE FUTURE

The integration of Artificial Intelligence (AI) into agriculture heralds a new era for farming, bringing forth innovations that promise to increase efficiency, sustainability, and productivity.

Precision Agriculture with AI

AI enhances farming practices through precision agriculture, optimizing resource use and boosting crop yields. By leveraging advanced algorithms and data analytics, AI aids in making precise decisions, reducing waste, and ensuring crops get precisely what they need for optimal growth.

AI-Driven Crop and Soil Monitoring

Crop health and soil conditions are critical for successful agriculture. AI-driven technologies, like deep convolutional neural networks, are being used to monitor these conditions closely. By analyzing images of crops and detecting signs of diseases or pests with high accuracy, AI provides actionable insights that can significantly improve farm productivity.

Automated Farming Machinery

The deployment of AI-powered drones and autonomous tractors is revolutionizing traditional farming methods. These machines perform tasks such as planting, weeding, and harvesting more efficiently and with less human labor. For example, overhead cameras and computer vision algorithms monitor cattle health, while UAVs equipped with AI can automate the precision spraying of pesticides or fertilizers.

Monetizing AI in Agriculture

The development and commercialization of AI-driven agricultural technologies offer vast opportunities for monetization. Strategies include software-as-a-service (SaaS) models, where farmers subscribe to use AI applications for crop monitoring or farm management and equipment leasing for AI-powered machinery. The increasing demand for such technologies is evident in the growing investment and adoption of AI solutions by the agricultural sector.

Companies like IBM and The Climate Corporation are at the forefront, providing AI-driven software for environmental intelligence and digital farming platforms, respectively. These tools help anticipate climate risks and manage farm operations efficiently, demonstrating the vast potential for AI in agriculture.

The future of farming with AI is not just about technological advancement but also about creating sustainable and efficient agricultural practices that can meet the growing global food demand. As we continue to embrace AI in agriculture, the sector is set to undergo a transformation that will benefit not only farmers but also the environment and the global community.

6.6: AI IN MANUFACTURING: EFFICIENCY AND PROFIT

The application of Artificial Intelligence (AI) in manufacturing marks a pivotal shift towards greater efficiency and profitability. Here's an overview of how AI is shaping the future of manufacturing:

Predictive Maintenance with AI

Predictive maintenance, powered by AI, enables the early detection of equipment failures, scheduling timely maintenance to avoid costly downtimes. MachineMetrics exemplifies this by diagnosing, predicting, and preventing machine tool failures, thus reducing scrap parts, quality issues, and downtime.

AI in Quality Control

AI revolutionizes quality control by employing machine vision and deep learning algorithms for real-time product inspection and defect identification. This not only ensures product quality but also minimizes waste and enhances workplace safety.

Supply Chain Optimization

AI plays a crucial role in optimizing manufacturing supply chains.

It improves inventory management, demand forecasting, and order fulfillment, thereby enhancing overall efficiency and profitability. AI tools analyze data from various sources, helping manufacturers to optimize inventory levels and reduce lead times.

Commercializing AI Solutions for Manufacturing

The commercialization of AI solutions in manufacturing opens up various monetization avenues, such as custom AI development and consulting services. AI solutions like Quantiphi empower manufacturers with data-driven intelligence, reducing manual effort and avoiding human error. Microsoft's AI solutions for manufacturing further illustrate the potential for AI to drive efficiencies across production and distribution processes.

For businesses looking to integrate AI into their manufacturing processes, tools like Asana, Teamwork, and WiPro offer varying functionalities to improve project management, supply chain optimization, and operational efficiencies.

As AI continues to evolve, its integration into manufacturing promises to streamline operations and foster innovation, driving the industry toward a more efficient, profitable, and sustainable future.

6.7: AI IN LOGISTICS AND SUPPLY CHAIN MANAGEMENT

The integration of Artificial Intelligence (AI) in logistics and supply chain management is revolutionizing the way companies plan, manage, and execute their operations. Let's delve into how AI is enhancing efficiency and creating new opportunities for innovation in this sector.

Route Optimization and Fleet Management

AI greatly enhances route optimization and fleet management by sifting through extensive data to identify the most efficient paths. This not only reduces fuel consumption and costs but also improves delivery times. Companies like Echo Global Logistics utilize AI to optimize transportation and logistics, ensuring goods are shipped quickly, securely, and cost-effectively.

Automated Warehousing Solutions

In warehousing, AI-powered robotics systems are streamlining inventory management and order fulfillment processes. Covariant showcases how autonomous robots equipped with AI can learn from each task, enhancing speed and reliability in warehousing operations. These robots can adapt to handling a wide range of objects and tasks, thereby improving operational efficiency.

Predictive Supply Chain Analytics

AI's predictive capabilities are crucial in forecasting supply chain disruptions, enabling businesses to manage these proactively. By analyzing diverse data sources, AI systems can predict potential risk events, allowing companies to save costs and avoid charges or penalties. For example, IBM leverages AI to monitor supply data and manage unforeseen delays with inbound deliveries.

Monetizing AI in Logistics

The development and commercialization of AI-driven logistics and supply chain management solutions offer significant monetization opportunities. By targeting e-commerce and retail industries, companies can offer services such as AI-based predictive analytics, automated warehousing solutions, and route optimization. This can include custom AI development, consulting services, and subscription-based models catering to the specific needs of these sectors.

With AI's ongoing evolution, its use in logistics and supply chain management is anticipated to grow, boosting efficiency, cutting operational expenses, and opening doors for new business models. However, the main hurdle lies in narrowing the gap between AI's potential and its actual application across businesses of various sizes.

CHAPTER 7
STEP-BY-STEP GUIDE TO YOUR FIRST AI PROJECT - BONUS

7.1 FINDING YOUR NICHE: HOW TO IDENTIFY PROFITABLE AI OPPORTUNITIES

Embarking on your first AI project can be both exciting and overwhelming. Identifying a specific area where AI can excel and provide substantial benefits is essential to achieving success. This section offers a comprehensive guide on discovering profitable AI opportunities.

Market Research Essentials

- **Understand Your Audience**: Begin by identifying the needs and challenges of your target audience. Collect valuable information by conducting surveys, interviews, and analyzing social media.
- **Analyze the Competition**: Look at existing solutions within your area of interest. Identify gaps and areas for improvement where AI could offer a competitive advantage.
- **Trend Analysis**: Leverage tools like Google Trends and industry reports to understand the market dynamics and the evolving needs within your niche.

Evaluating AI's Impact

- **Scalability and Sustainability**: Assess potential AI solutions for their scalability. Can they handle growing data volumes and user interactions over time?
- **Value Proposition**: Consider how AI can uniquely address the challenges identified in your market research, creating a solid value proposition.
- **ROI Estimation**: Evaluate the potential return on investment for your AI solution, considering development costs, operational expenses, and possible revenue streams.

Case Studies of Success

- Highlight stories of individuals or companies successfully implementing niche AI projects, resulting in significant passive income. Analyze their strategies, from conception through execution, focusing on the AI technologies utilized and the market needs they addressed.

Tools and Resources for Niche Identification

- **Google Keyword Planner**: To understand search trends and demands for potential AI applications.
- **CB Insights**: Offers insights into emerging AI trends and startups, providing a glimpse into where investment and innovation are heading.
- **TechCrunch**: Regularly features new and innovative applications of AI across different industries, which can inspire niche ideas.

Following these steps and leveraging the listed tools and resources can help you systematically uncover and evaluate profitable AI opportunities. Remember, the goal is to find a niche where AI technology can solve real problems, create value, and sustain long-term growth.

1. **Google Keyword Planner**: Accessible through the Google Ads platform, this tool helps identify search trends and

keyword ideas for your niche. Visit: **https://ads.google.-com/home/tools/keyword-planner/**

2. **CB Insights**: Known for analyzing emerging tech, investments, and startups, including AI. Find detailed reports and articles at their official website: **https://www.cbinsights.com/**

3. **TechCrunch**: Offers the latest technology news and information about startups, including those in the AI sector. You can find inspiring stories and AI application examples at **https://techcrunch.com/**

7.2 THE BLUEPRINT: PLANNING YOUR FIRST AI PROJECT

Creating a successful AI project requires careful planning and execution. This section will guide you through setting objectives, designing your AI solution, budgeting, and assessing risks to ensure your project's success.

Setting Clear Objectives

- **Define Specific Goals**: Define what you want your AI project to achieve. Whether it's automating a specific task, enhancing customer experience, or generating new insights, clear objectives will guide your project's direction.
- **Measurable Outcomes**: Ensure your goals are measurable. For example, aim to improve process efficiency by a certain percentage or achieve a specific revenue target within a set period.

Designing Your AI Solution

- **Identify the Problem**: Clearly articulate the problem your AI solution aims to solve. This ensures the solution is tailored to meet specific needs.
- **Choose the Right Tools and Technologies**: Select AI tools and technologies best suited to your project. Consider factors like scalability, ease of integration, and community support.

- **Prototype and Iterate**: Develop a prototype of your solution and test it with potential users. Gather feedback and refine your approach accordingly.

Budgeting and Resource Allocation

- **Estimate Costs**: List all potential costs associated with your AI project, including software, cloud computing resources, and data acquisition.
- **Plan for Scalability**: Consider future scaling needs in your budget. Initial cost-saving measures should maintain the ability to grow your solution.
- **Seek Funding if Necessary**: Explore funding options such as angel investors, venture capital, or grants for technology innovation if your project requires significant investment.

Risk Assessment and Mitigation

- **Identify Risks**: Assess potential risks, including technical challenges, data privacy concerns, and market acceptance.
- **Develop a Risk Mitigation Plan**: Develop strategies to mitigate each identified risk. These could include contingency plans, investing in security measures, or conducting market research.

This blueprint serves as a foundation for planning and executing an AI project, focusing on clear objectives, strategic design, prudent budgeting, and comprehensive risk management. Following these guidelines will help ensure your AI project is well-positioned for success.

As this guidance is based on standard project management and AI development practices, I recommend consulting specific resources such as AI project management tools, cloud computing platforms, and data privacy frameworks for detailed information—websites like **https://cloud.google.com**, **https://aws.amazon.com**, and **https://www.microsoft.com/en-us/ai** provide extensive documentation and tools for AI project development.

Additionally, **https://www.projectmanagement.com** offers resources on project management techniques applicable to AI projects.

7.3 ACQUIRING AND PREPARING YOUR DATA: THE FUEL FOR AI

The success of an AI project heavily relies on the quality and quantity of the data it uses. This section delves into understanding data needs, collection methods, preparation techniques, and the crucial aspects of data privacy and ethics.

Understanding Data Needs

- **Types of Data**: Different AI projects require different types of data. For instance, machine learning models might need labeled datasets for training, while natural language processing (NLP) projects could require large amounts of textual data.
- **Impact on Planning**: The required data type influences many aspects of project planning, including the tools you'll use, the time investment for data collection and preparation, and the overall approach to model training.

Data Collection Methods

- **Public Datasets**: Many organizations release datasets for research and development purposes. Websites like Kaggle (**https://www.kaggle.com/datasets**) and Google Dataset Search (**https://datasetsearch.research.google.com/**) are great places to look for existing datasets.
- **Web Scraping**: Tools like Beautiful Soup and Scrapy allow for automated data collection from web pages. However, it's crucial to comply with website terms of use and legal restrictions.
- **Partnerships**: Collaborating with organizations with the needed data can be beneficial. Ensure agreements respect data privacy laws and ethical guidelines.

Data Cleaning and Preparation

- **Cleaning**: The process of data cleansing involves the elimination of errors and inconsistencies from your data. This step is essential for enhancing the precision of AI predictions.
- **Preparation**: Includes tasks like normalization, transformation, and feature selection to make the data more suitable for modeling.

Data Privacy and Ethics

- **Legal Compliance**: Familiarize yourself with laws governing the use of personal data, such as GDPR in Europe and CCPA in California.
- **Ethical Considerations**: Go beyond legal requirements by considering the impact of your data collection and usage on individuals' privacy and societal norms.

In summary, data is the backbone of AI projects and determines their potential success. Understanding your data needs, effectively collecting and preparing your data, and adhering to privacy and ethical standards are fundamental steps in any AI project. This approach ensures the technical viability of your AI solutions and builds trust and compliance with global standards.

7.4 SELECTING THE RIGHT AI TOOLS FOR YOUR PROJECT

The selection of appropriate AI tools and platforms is critical for the success of your project. This chapter provides an overview of the landscape, factors to consider when choosing tools, a comparison of open-source versus commercial options, and recommendations based on user reviews and use cases.

Overview of AI Tools and Platforms

AI tools and platforms offer a range of functionalities, from data analysis and machine learning model development to deployment and monitoring. Each tool has its strengths and is suited to particular use cases:

- **Data Analysis and Preprocessing Tools**: Ideal for cleaning and preparing your data for modeling.
- **Machine Learning Frameworks**: You can use powerful tools like TensorFlow or PyTorch to create and teach complex models.
- **AI Development Platforms**: Offer integrated services to streamline AI application development, deployment, and scaling.

Criteria for Tool Selection

Selecting the right AI tool for your project involves considering several criteria:

- **Ease of Use**: Tools that offer intuitive interfaces and extensive documentation can significantly reduce the learning curve.
- **Scalability**: The tool should be able to scale with your project's growing needs without significant changes to the infrastructure.
- **Community Support**: A strong community can provide valuable resources, from troubleshooting to best practices.

Open Source vs. Commercial Tools

- **Open Source Tools**: Offer flexibility and no upfront cost. The community continually improves them, but support can be limited.
- **Commercial Tools**: Often come with dedicated support and advanced features that are out of the box but at a financial cost.

Recommendations and Reviews

Here are five AI tools showcasing a mix of open-source and

commercial options, each suited for different aspects of AI project development:

1. **TensorFlow**: A community-supported framework for developing neural networks and machine learning known for its flexibility and open-source nature.
2. **PyTorch**: Favoured for its ease of use and dynamic computation graph, making it ideal for research and prototyping.
3. **IBM Watson**: A commercial platform offering robust AI services and tools for businesses, known for its natural language processing capabilities.
4. **Google Cloud AI**: It offers a range of artificial intelligence services and application programming interfaces designed to address various AI use cases, such as speech recognition and natural language comprehension.
5. **Microsoft Azure AI**: Offers a comprehensive set of AI tools and services, including machine learning, knowledge mining, and AI services for developers to build intelligent solutions.

7.5: STEP-BY-STEP: SETTING UP YOUR FIRST AI MODEL

Embarking on your AI journey requires understanding the fundamentals of AI model development. This chapter guides you through setting up your first AI model, from selection to continuous improvement.

When selecting AI tools, consider starting with user reviews and case studies to understand how they have been applied in similar projects. Websites like GitHub for open-source projects or G2 for commercial product reviews can provide valuable insights from current users.

Selecting the right AI tools and platforms is pivotal in steering your project toward its objectives efficiently and effectively. When making your choice, consider your project's specific needs, budget, and the level of support you require.

Choosing the Right Model

Selecting the most suitable AI model for your project is pivotal. Factors to consider include the model's accuracy, efficiency, and complexity relative to your project's goals. For instance, a simpler model might suffice for fundamental data analysis, while complex projects like image or speech recognition demand more sophisticated models.

Model Training Basics

Training an AI model involves setting parameters and feeding it data to learn from. This process optimizes the model's accuracy by adjusting its weights based on input data and intended output. Essential libraries for this include **pandas** for data manipulation, **matplotlib** for plotting, and various **sklearn** modules for model training and evaluation.

Validating Your Model

Validating your AI model's performance is crucial to ensure it meets the desired objectives. This might involve using metrics like accuracy score for classification tasks or mean squared error for regression tasks. Techniques include splitting your dataset into training and testing sets or using cross-validation methods to evaluate model performance on unseen data.

Iterations and Improvements

Iterative improvements based on feedback and changing data or objectives are essential for refining your AI model. This could involve adjusting parameters, adding more data, or changing the model structure. Tools like Keras allow for easy model adjustments and testing with different activation functions and layer configurations to enhance performance.

AI Tools and Platforms for Online Course Automation

- **Plat.AI** provides a comprehensive guide to building AI, from identifying the problem to picking the right platform, whether in-house frameworks like Tensorflow and PyTorch or cloud frameworks for faster deployment.
- **The Code Dose** offers a step-by-step guide on creating AI chatbots using Python and the OpenAI API, illustrating the process from installing the necessary packages to creating interactive chat functions.

- **Elegant Themes** discusses Chatbase, a tool that facilitates the uploading and structuring of data for AI chatbots. It also allows for fine-tuning AI with prompt engineering for more targeted and effective user interactions.

For more detailed insights into setting up your first AI model, including practical examples and guides, the following resources are invaluable:

- Machine Learning Mastery's Python tutorials, Your First Machine Learning Project and Your First Deep Learning Project, offer step-by-step guides for starting with machine learning and deep learning projects.
- Plat.AI's How to Build an AI provides a structured approach to AI development, from problem identification to platform selection.
- The Code Dose's Creating Your First AI Chatbot Using Python explains the process of developing an AI chatbot with OpenAI's API.
- Elegant Themes' guide on Making Your Own AI discusses data handling and fine-tuning AI models for chatbots.

For comprehensive guidance on setting up your first AI model, including practical examples and in-depth tutorials, the following resources are invaluable:

- **Machine Learning Mastery** Python-based guides presented in a step-by-step format are available for individuals interested in beginning projects related to machine learning and deep learning.
- **Plat.AI** provides a structured approach to AI development, from problem identification to selecting the right platform, whether it's in-house frameworks like TensorFlow and PyTorch or cloud platforms for faster deployment. Learn more at https://plat.ai.
- **The Code Dose** explains the process of developing an AI chatbot with OpenAI's API, from installing the necessary

packages to creating interactive chat functions. Detailed
steps can be found at https://thecodedose.com.

- **Elegant Themes** offers insights into creating your AI,
  focusing on data handling and fine-tuning AI models for
  chatbots. Discover more at https://www.elegantthemes.-
  com/blog/technology/how-to-make-your-own-ai.

These resources offer valuable perspectives on utilizing AI for
various applications, guiding you through the complexities of AI
model development, training, and application with clear, actionable
instructions.

7.6 TRAINING YOUR AI: TIPS AND TRICKS FOR BEGINNERS

As you embark on your journey of integrating artificial intelligence
into your online money-making strategies, understanding the nuances
of AI model training is crucial. Below, you'll find guidance on optimizing your AI model training, handling common issues such as overfitting and underfitting, leveraging pre-trained models, and utilizing
collaborative resources.

Optimizing Model Training

- **Speed and Accuracy**: Enhance your training process by
  selecting appropriate algorithms and using hardware
  acceleration (e.g., GPUs) where possible. Techniques like
  batch normalization and dropout can also improve training
  speed and model accuracy.

Handling Overfitting and Underfitting

- **Balancing the Model**: Address overfitting by simplifying the
  model or applying regularization techniques. For
  underfitting, consider increasing model complexity or the
  volume of training data.

Using Pre-trained Models

- **Efficiency and Customization**: Utilize models pre-trained on large datasets to save time. Fine-tune these models to your specific needs for improved performance with less computational resource requirement.

Collaborative Training Resources

- **Community and Platforms**: Engage with platforms like GitHub or specialized AI forums where you can share and gain insights on model training, datasets, and troubleshooting.

AI Tools for AI Projects:

To further assist your learning and development in AI, here are five recommended AI tools:

1. **TensorFlow** (www.tensorflow.org): A comprehensive, open-source platform that facilitates the development of machine learning and deep learning models.
2. **Scikit-learn** (www.scikit-learn.org): Python Library is designed to offer users simple yet powerful tools to analyze and mine data. Its main objective is to provide an effective way to perform data analysis and mining. The software is designed to be accessible to all and suited for various purposes.
3. **PyTorch** (www.pytorch.org): An open-source machine learning library based on the Torch library, known for its flexibility and speed.
4. **Keras** (keras.io): This is a Python-based neural networks API that works with TensorFlow, CNTK, or Theano. It operates at a high level and can be used for various purposes.
5. **OpenCV** (opencv.org): Focused on real-time computer vision applications, it's widely used for face detection and object identification tasks.

The functionalities provided by these tools range from data

processing and model building to deployment. These tools are designed to cater to beginners as well as experienced practitioners in the field of AI. By utilizing these tools and adhering to the outlined tips and tricks, you'll be well on your way to successfully training your AI models and leveraging artificial intelligence in your online endeavors

7.7 TESTING AND TWEAKING: REFINING YOUR AI MODEL

The journey from developing an AI model to its successful deployment involves rigorous testing and fine-tuning. This chapter dives into the essentials of refining your AI models through testing strategies, interpreting results, fine-tuning techniques, and understanding when to pivot.

Testing Strategies

Practical testing of AI models includes employing various strategies to ensure robustness and reliability. Techniques like **cross-validation** help assess how the model will generalize to an independent dataset. **Real-world testing** is crucial for observing the model's performance in practical scenarios. Tools such as Testsigma, Katalon Studio, and Applitools leverage AI to enhance test automation, offering capabilities like visual testing, plain English test automation, and AI-powered checks for various applications.

Interpreting Test Results

Understanding test results is critical to identifying areas for improvement. It involves analyzing accuracy, precision, recall, and other relevant metrics to gauge the model's performance. Visual validation tools, for example, use AI's pattern recognition capabilities to detect visual bugs, ensuring that all visual elements function correctly and are engaging.

Fine-tuning Techniques

Fine-tuning your AI model can significantly improve its performance. This may include adjusting hyperparameters, incorporating additional data, or using techniques like transfer learning, where a pre-trained model is adapted for a new but related problem. Tools such as DeepChecks provide an open-source framework for testing ML models and data, enabling various checks throughout the ML pipeline to ensure data integrity, validation, and model testing.

When to Pivot

Recognizing when a project is not viable in its current form is crucial. Indicators include consistently poor performance metrics, inability to generalize to new data, or excessive complexity with minimal gains. Pivoting may involve changing the model architecture, data preprocessing techniques, or even redefining the problem statement.

For a more in-depth exploration and resources on AI testing tools and strategies, Testsigma's platform might be useful for a wide range of testing needs.

7.8 LAUNCHING YOUR AI PROJECT: A BEGINNER'S CHECKLIST

Launching your AI project marks a pivotal moment in its development lifecycle. It's the transition from theory and development into real-world application. To ensure a smooth transition and the successful implementation of your AI project, follow this comprehensive guide tailored for beginners.

Pre-launch Checklist

Before unveiling your AI project to the public, ensuring that every aspect is thoroughly vetted and ready for deployment is essential. Here's a checklist to guide you through the critical pre-launch phase:

- **Functionality Testing**: Verify that all components of your AI system work as intended.
- **Performance Evaluation**: Ensure your AI model performs efficiently under different conditions and scales appropriately.
- **Security Measures**: Implement robust security protocols to protect your data and users' privacy.
- **User Experience (UX) Assessment**: Test the user interface and experience to ensure it's intuitive and user-friendly.
- **Compliance and Ethical Considerations**: Ensure your AI project meets relevant regulations and ethical guidelines.

Launching Strategies

Launching an AI project requires careful planning and strategic execution. Here are some strategies to consider:

- **Soft Launch**: Begin with a limited release to a select audience. This will allow you to collect early feedback and make any required changes.
- **Beta Testing**: Invite users to test your AI project in its beta stage. This phase is crucial for identifying bugs and understanding user experience from a broader audience.
- **Phased Rollout**: Gradually release your AI project to larger audiences, allowing for manageable adjustments and scalability assessments.

Monitoring and Support

The work doesn't stop after launch. Continuous monitoring and support are key to the ongoing success of your AI project.

- **Real-time Monitoring**: Utilize tools to monitor the performance and health of your AI system constantly.
- **User Support**: Provide clear channels for users to report issues or seek help. Consider FAQs, live chat support, or user forums.
- **Regular Updates**: Keep your AI project fresh and relevant with regular updates, incorporating the latest advancements in AI technology.

Gathering and Incorporating Feedback

Feedback is invaluable for the iterative improvement of your AI project.

- **Feedback Channels**: Establish multiple channels for feedback collection, such as surveys, user interviews, and analytics.
- **Analyzing Feedback**: Systematically analyze the feedback to identify patterns and areas for improvement.

- **Iterative Development**: Use the insights gained from feedback to make informed enhancements to your AI project.

By adhering to this checklist and embracing a strategic approach to the launch and beyond, you're setting your AI project up for a successful introduction and sustained growth. Remember, success is not just about launching your project. It requires ongoing engagement, monitoring, and adaptation, which are crucial for long-term success.

7.9 MEASURING SUCCESS: UNDERSTANDING AI PERFORMANCE METRICS

Evaluating the success of your AI project is crucial for understanding its impact and guiding future improvements. This chapter focuses on critical aspects of measuring and leveraging your AI project's success.

Key Performance Indicators (KPIs)

Assessing the effectiveness of your AI project is crucial, and KPIs play a significant role in achieving this. Essential KPIs include accuracy, efficiency, user engagement, and cost savings. Identifying the right KPIs involves understanding your project's goals and the specific metrics that best reflect its success.

Benchmarking Your AI Project

Benchmarking involves comparing your AI project's performance against industry standards or competitors. This process helps identify where your project stands in the market and uncovers areas for improvement. Tools like Tableau and Salesforce offer analytics and business intelligence features to aid in this process, providing insights into market trends and competitor performance.

Continuous Improvement Process

An iterative approach to improvement based on performance metrics ensures your AI project remains competitive. Review your KPIs regularly, gather data, and analyze results to identify trends and areas for enhancement. Platforms such as H2O.ai and Oracle AI offer machine learning capabilities to analyze performance data and automate insights for improvement.

Leveraging Success for Growth

The success of your AI project can be a catalyst for further growth. Strategies include scaling up operations, exploring new markets, or diversifying your AI applications. Success stories and positive performance metrics can attract investors, partnerships, and customers, driving your project's expansion.

AI Tools for Performance Measurement

To support the measurement and enhancement of your AI project, consider leveraging the following AI tools:

1. **Fireflies**: Automates meeting transcription and analysis, integrating with popular platforms like Zoom and Google Meets.
2. **Midjourney**: Provides AI-driven image creation, enabling rich visual content for marketing and project presentations.
3. **DALL-E 2 by OpenAI:** Another AI image generator that translates text prompts into images, aiding in creating visual content.
4. **Tome**: An AI storytelling partner that generates presentations from prompts, useful for summarizing project outcomes and strategies.
5. **Lumen5**: Facilitates quick video creation, which can be used for project demonstrations or marketing materials.

Utilizing these tools can enhance how you measure, analyze, and present your AI project's performance, ensuring ongoing improvement and leveraging success for further growth.

7.10 SCALING UP: EXPANDING YOUR AI PROJECTS FOR GREATER INCOME

This crucial chapter delves into effective methodologies for scaling AI projects to enhance their income-generating potential. By adopting a strategic approach, businesses can navigate the complexities of expansion while optimizing their AI applications for success. The insights provided here draw from various sources to present a comprehensive guide.

- **Identifying Scalability Opportunities**: Recognizing the potential for scaling your AI project is foundational. This involves understanding the market demand, the scalability of the AI technology itself, and identifying areas where your AI solution can deliver enhanced value.
- **Strategies for Scaling AI Projects**: Effective scaling strategies may include technological advancements, leveraging cloud computing for enhanced computational power, expanding into new markets, or diversifying the application of your AI project to cater to broader use cases.
- **Managing Increased Complexity**: With growth comes complexity. Expanding your team, incorporating more robust project management processes, and optimizing your AI models for scalability are essential steps. This might involve investing in more sophisticated AI tools or platforms that facilitate efficient scaling.
- **Sustaining Growth**: Long-term growth requires continuous innovation and adaptation. Staying abreast of the latest AI trends, engaging with your user base for feedback, and iterating on your project based on real-world performance is vital for sustained success.

To aid in these efforts, exploring the latest AI tools is essential. Here are five examples of game-changing AI tools that can support the scaling of AI projects:

1. **Fireflies.ai**: An AI tool for meeting transcription and analysis, offering automated meeting recordings, transcriptions, and notes integration with popular platforms like Zoom and Google Meets.
2. **Midjourney**: A top-tier AI tool for image generation, allowing the creation of images in various styles through simple prompts.
3. **DALL-E 2**: Developed by OpenAI, this AI image generator transforms text prompts into images, supporting creative project scalability.

4. **Tome**: An AI-powered presentation builder that generates
   text, images, and slides for presentations, facilitating efficient
   content creation.
5. **Lumen5:** Specializes in AI-powered video creation, offering
   a simple interface for quick video production. It is ideal for
   scaling marketing and promotional content.

Each of these tools embodies the potential to significantly enhance the scalability of AI projects, from automating mundane tasks to fostering creative output and efficient project management. Embracing such technologies can streamline operations, reduce overheads, and unlock new avenues for income generation.

STEP INTO THE FUTURE OF FINANCE WITH THE AI WEALTH ENTREPRENEUR PROGRAM

Dear AI Wealth Entrepreneur,

As the dawn of the artificial intelligence era redefines what's possible, the key to unlocking a new dimension of financial freedom is within your grasp. Fueled by the insights from "The Age of AI Wealth," it's time to elevate your financial game to unprecedented heights. Welcome to the gateway of transformation: The AI Wealth Entrepreneur Program.

This program isn't merely a course; it's your roadmap to leveraging AI's power for extraordinary wealth creation. Imagine utilizing the intelligence of machines to explore and conquer new realms of investment, wealth management, and financial innovation.

Your Journey with Us Offers Unparalleled Benefits:

- **Deep Dives into AI's Financial Impact**: Explore AI's transformative role in wealth with in-depth analyses and pioneering case studies.
- **Actionable Wealth Growth Strategies**: Move from insight to impact with concrete steps to integrate AI into your financial strategies.
- **Exclusive Access to AI Financial Tools**: Harness our specially developed AI tools and methodologies designed to amplify your financial growth.

- **Community of Creators**: Join forces with a network of forward-thinking individuals, all poised to lead in tomorrow's financial landscape.

For those determined to not just navigate but lead in the financial future, the AI Wealth Entrepreneur Program is your foundation for success.

Join the Waitlist: Secure Your FREE Spot Today

The future belongs to those who prepare for it today. Don't let another moment pass in uncertainty. Embrace the promise of AI and step into a world of endless financial possibilities with the AI Wealth Entrepreneur Program.

"In the era of AI, your wealth is not just counted in currency, but in the innovative ways you choose to earn, grow, and manage it. Your Money is AI. Make it Revolutionary."

Do not let the future pass you by. Seize the moment with AI, and embark on your journey to financial excellence with the AI Wealth Entrepreneur Program.

Ready to Redefine What Wealth Means?

Join us now and pave your way to an AI-enhanced prosperous future. Spaces are limited, and demand is high. Ensure you don't miss this transformative opportunity by joining our waitlist now. For access and the chance to redefine your financial destiny, click on the link below:

https://aiwealthentrepreneur.com/waitlistprogram

or scan the QR code:

Dare to redefine your financial future? Click through and let the journey to unparalleled prosperity begin.

To your limitless potential!

UNLOCK YOUR FINANCIAL POTENTIAL: SPECIAL FREE BONUS

Dear AI Wealth Entrepreneur,

Congratulations on taking the first step towards unlocking a world where your financial destiny is not just a dream but a reality you can actively shape. As you embark on this transformative journey with the AI Wealth Entrepreneur Program, we have a special surprise to further fuel your path to success.

Introducing Your Bonus Gift: "Passive Income Ideas For Beginners" by Morgan Powers

In our commitment to providing you with unparalleled resources to accelerate your wealth-building journey, I'm thrilled to offer you an exclusive bonus. Receive a complimentary copy of "Passive Income Ideas For Beginners: Discover The Best Ways to Make Money Online From Home and Gain Financial Freedom," a comprehensive guide by the renowned author Morgan Powers.

This invaluable e-book is your roadmap to creating streams of passive income that empower you to earn on your own terms. Whether you desire the flexibility to work when and where you want or you're aiming to diversify your income sources, this book is the key to unlocking your potential.

- **A Beginner-Friendly Blueprint**: Step into the world of online entrepreneurship with ease. This guide is crafted for beginners, offering a clear pathway from concept to execution.
- **15 Unique Online Business Ideas**: Explore a curated selection of online business models that promise not only profitability but also scalability and accessibility, regardless of your experience level.
- **Low Start-Up Costs, High Scalability**: Learn how to launch and grow your business with minimal initial investment, maximizing your return on investment.
- **Diverse Income Streams**: From affiliate marketing to digital product creation, real estate investing to social media management, uncover a variety of avenues to generate income online.
- **Expert Insights and Strategies**: Morgan Powers shares the most effective methods for building a reliable and lucrative online business, helping you find your niche and succeed.

Your Path to Independence

"Passive Income Ideas For Beginners" is more than a book; it's a companion in your journey to financial independence. It underscores a crucial message: You don't have to be tied to a traditional job to achieve wealth and success. The digital age offers limitless opportunities to those willing to explore and invest in new income streams.

Download Your Free E-Book Now

Embrace this opportunity to equip yourself with knowledge that could change your life. Access your complimentary copy of "Passive Income Ideas For Beginners" by clicking the link below or scan the QR code:

https://aiwealthentrepreneur.com/morgan

Additionally, if you prefer reading on your Kindle, this book is also available on Amazon. You can purchase it using the following link:

https://www.amazon.com/dp/B094GFFKV8

Take this step towards freedom and success. Let this book be the start of an incredible journey to achieving the financial independence you deserve.

To your unstoppable success!

AFTERWORD

As I draw this journey to a close, I've traversed from the foundational understanding of Artificial Intelligence (AI) to leveraging its vast potential for creating not just income streams but also for crafting innovative pathways to financial freedom. This book has guided you through the intricacies of AI, demystifying its components, and showcasing how it can be a formidable ally in building wealth.

I began by laying the foundation for understanding AI, exploring the basics and the brain behind AI—machine learning. Along the way, I decoded essential AI jargon and traced its evolution from a theoretical concept to everyday applications. I examined how AI is revolutionizing industries globally and discussed the importance of balancing innovation with responsibility.

Understanding AI's role in digital marketing was pivotal, as I explored how it can personalize customer experiences, enhance content creation from blogging to vlogging, and revolutionize email marketing. I also delved into using AI to optimize websites, analyze competitors, and improve customer service through AI chatbots.

Creating multiple passive income streams with AI became a central theme, covering everything from AI-driven affiliate marketing and selling AI-created digital products to enhancing e-commerce sales and automating online courses. I also explored the intersection of AI and art, including graphic design, writing, music composition, and game development, demonstrating how AI can unleash creativity and generate new income opportunities.

In addition to these primary areas, I ventured into the broader applications of AI, such as its impact on real estate, healthcare, personal finance management, agriculture, manufacturing, and logistics. Each of these sectors showcased AI's potential to streamline operations, enhance efficiency, and open new avenues for innovation.

To ensure you could take actionable steps, I provided a step-by-step guide to your first AI project, covering everything from finding your niche and planning your project to training and launching your AI model. This hands-on approach aimed to transform theoretical knowledge into practical success.

Anyone can make money online with artificial intelligence in just 30 minutes a day if you master the tools and follow the guidelines outlined in this book. The advancements in AI technology have democratized access to powerful resources that can automate tasks, optimize strategies, and generate income streams with minimal time investment. By leveraging the tools and techniques discussed, you can effectively harness AI to create and grow your online business. Whether you are new to the field or an experienced entrepreneur, dedicating a small portion of your day to implementing these strategies can lead to significant financial gains. Remember, consistency and dedication to mastering these tools are key to unlocking the full potential of AI in your online ventures.

Your story is invaluable. I encourage you to share your adventures, triumphs, and learnings within the community. Whether through a dedicated hashtag or an online forum, your narrative can enlighten and inspire, contributing to a collective wealth of knowledge.

As we stand on the brink of further AI breakthroughs, the potential for revolutionizing financial independence continues to expand. You are now equipped to navigate this evolving landscape, poised at the vanguard of leveraging AI for financial autonomy.

Thank you for embarking on this exploratory journey into AI and its financial possibilities. Your dedication to understanding and applying AI principles is commendable. Here's to your success in using AI to carve paths to financial freedom. May your journey be fruitful and your endeavors prosperous.

END-OF-BOOK REVIEW PAGE

Title: Keeping the Dream Thriving

You've just unlocked the secrets of leveraging AI for financial success, and now, it's time to help others discover this valuable resource.

By sharing your thoughts on Amazon, you're not just leaving a review; you're helping fellow dreamers find the key to unlocking their potential in the digital age.

Your support is invaluable. The mission to make online earning accessible to everyone relies on the collective sharing of knowledge, and your contribution is crucial.

Your review will light the way for many others, guiding them on their path to financial independence. Together, we can keep the dream of achieving financial freedom alive for all.

Just scan the QR code or clicking the link below and share your thoughts:

https://www.amazon.com/review/review-your-purchases/?asin=191734001X

Thank you for being a vital part of this journey.

BOOK REWARDS

Join the BOOK rewards program today and start earning as you read! Simply scan the QR code:

or click:

https://earnbookrewards.com/subscribe

to sign up.

Once you're a member, you can start accumulating BOOK coins. Don't miss out on this exciting opportunity to make your reading experience even more rewarding!

Five secret words:
1. Bookrewards
2. Pageturner
3. Chaptermaster
4. Bookseeker
5. Readstory

BIBLIOGRAPHY

Chapter 1

1. Scribbr. (n.d.). *Glossary of AI Terms | Acronyms & Terminology*. Scribbr. Retrieved from https://www.scribbr.com/ai/glossary-of-ai-terms/
2. Wikipedia contributors. (n.d.). Glossary of artificial intelligence. In *Wikipedia, The Free Encyclopedia*. Retrieved from https://en.wikipedia.org/wiki/Glossary_of_artificial_intelligence
3. TechTarget. (n.d.). *The History of Artificial Intelligence: Complete AI Timeline*. Retrieved from https://www.techtarget.com
4. Science in the News, Harvard University. (n.d.). *The History of Artificial Intelligence*. Retrieved from https://sitn.hms.harvard.edu
5. Wikipedia contributors. (n.d.). Artificial intelligence. In *Wikipedia, The Free Encyclopedia*. Retrieved from https://en.wikipedia.org/wiki/Artificial_intelligence
6. McCulloch, W.S., & Pitts, W. (1943). "A Logical Calculus of Ideas Immanent in Nervous Activity."
7. Turing, A.M. (1950). "Computing Machinery and Intelligence." Mind, 59, 433-460.
8. Dartmouth Conference (1956). "Proposal for the Dartmouth Summer Research Project on Artificial Intelligence."
9. Rosenblatt, F. (1958). "The Perceptron: A Probabilistic Model for Information Storage and Organization in the Brain." Psychological Review, 65, 386-408.
10. McCarthy, J. (1960). "Recursive Functions of Symbolic Expressions and Their Computation by Machine, Part I." Communications of the ACM, 3(4), 184-195.
11. Samuel, A.L. (1959). "Some Studies in Machine Learning Using the Game of Checkers." IBM Journal of Research and Development, 3(3), 210-229.
12. Weizenbaum, J. (1966). "ELIZA—A Computer Program for the Study of Natural Language Communication Between Man and Machine." Communications of the ACM, 9(1), 36-45.
13. WABOT-1 (1970). "Introduction of WABOT-1: The World's First Humanoid Robot."
14. IBM Deep Blue (1997). "Deep Blue Defeats Garry Kasparov."
15. iRobot Roomba (2002). "Introduction of the Roomba Autonomous Vacuum Cleaner."
16. OpenAI Dactyl (2019). "Dactyl AI System Solves Rubik's Cube."
17. Google Duplex (2018). "Google Duplex: An AI System for Natural Conversations."
18. Wikipedia. "Timeline of artificial intelligence."
19. AI Navigator. "AI Timeline: Key Events in Artificial Intelligence from 1950-2024."
20. AIBriefingRoom. "The Evolution Of Artificial Intelligence: A Timeline."
21. Caspa.ai. "A Comprehensive Timeline of AI: Past, Present & Future."
22. World Economic Forum. (2023, December). *Life after the hype: How AI is transforming industries and economies*. Retrieved from https://www.weforum.org/agenda/2023/12/life-after-the-hype-how-ai-is-transforming-industries-and-economies/
23. Microsoft News. (n.d.). *The global impact of AI across industries*. Retrieved from https://news.microsoft.com/transform/the-global-impact-of-ai-across-industries/

24. UNESCO. (n.d.). *Ethics of Artificial Intelligence*. Retrieved from https://www.unesco.org

25. World Economic Forum. (2021, June). *Ethical principles for AI*. Retrieved from https://www.weforum.org/agenda/2021/06/ethical-principles-for-ai/

26. Knowledge at Wharton. (n.d.). *What's Your Company's AI Readiness Quotient?* Retrieved from https://knowledge.wharton.upenn.edu

27. Tesseract Academy. (n.d.). *Assessing your Organization's AI Readiness Level*. Retrieved from https://tesseract.academy

28. Emerj Artificial Intelligence Research. (n.d.). *How to Build an Enterprise AI Roadmap – A Four-Step Process*. Retrieved from https://emerj.com

29. McKinsey & Company. (n.d.). *The real-world potential and limitations of artificial intelligence*. Retrieved from https://www.mckinsey.com

30. Datanami. (n.d.). *Understanding AI's Limitations Is Key to Unlocking Its Potential*. Retrieved from https://www.datanami.com

31. McKinsey & Company. (n.d.). *What AI can and can't do (yet) for your business*. Retrieved from https://www.mckinsey.com

Chapter 2

1. Udemy. "ChatGPT Masterclass: ChatGPT Guide for Beginners to Experts!" Retrieved from Udemy

2. Search Engine Journal. (2023). "History Of ChatGPT: A Timeline Of Generative AI Chatbots." Retrieved from searchenginejournal.com

3. 365 Data Science. (2023). "The Evolution of ChatGPT: History and Future." Retrieved from 365datascience.com

4. Nature. (2023). "ChatGPT one year on: who is using it, how and why?" Retrieved from nature.com

5. Office Timeline. (2023). "Artificial Intelligence (AI) and ChatGPT timelines." Retrieved from officetimeline.com

6. Descript. "100+ ChatGPT prompts for creators: Speed up your workflow with AI." Retrieved from descript.com

7. Udemy. "The Ultimate Guide to ChatGPT for Content Creators." Retrieved from Udemy

8. Microsoft Create. "AI + you: How to use ChatGPT for content creation." Retrieved from create.microsoft.com

9. Skillshare. "Unlock your Creative Potential with AI: ChatGPT for Content Creators." Retrieved from skillshare.com

10. Montti, R. (2024, February 8). "Research Shows That Offering Tips To ChatGPT Improves Responses." *Search Engine Journal*. Retrieved from searchenginejournal.com

11. AnoE. (2023, August 4). "Does saying 'please' and 'thank you' to LLMs change anything?" *GenAI Stack Exchange*. Retrieved from genai.stackexchange.com

12. Chat-Prompt.com. (2024, March 20). "6 Proven ChatGPT Prompts: Developing thank-you notes." Retrieved from chat-prompt.com

13. OpenAI. (2023). "ChatGPT Pricing." Retrieved from openai.com

14. Microsoft. (2023). "Microsoft 365 Pricing." Retrieved from microsoft.com

15. Google. (2023). "Google Cloud AI Pricing." Retrieved from cloud.google.com

16. Anthropic. (2023). "Claude 3: Overview and Pricing." Retrieved from anthropic.com

Chapter 3

1.   Wix. (n.d.). The digital gold rush: how to make money with AI. Retrieved from https://www.wix.com/blog/how-to-make-money-with-ai

2.   Plain English. (n.d.). Insights into using AI for different passive income streams. Retrieved from https://www.plainenglish.io

3.   Ippei Blog. (n.d.). Strategies for generating passive income through AI. Retrieved from https://ippei.com

4.   Elegant Themes. (n.d.). AI tools for enhancing digital marketing efforts and generating passive income. Retrieved from https://www.elegantthemes.com

5.   GOBankingRates. (n.d.). Ways AI can be applied to create passive income opportunities. Retrieved from https://www.gobankingrates.com

6.   Geeky Gadgets. (n.d.). 25+ AI passive income ideas and strategies. Retrieved from https://www.geeky-gadgets.com

7.   Jasper.ai. (n.d.). Tools for content creation and enhancing affiliate marketing efforts with AI. Retrieved from https://www.jasper.ai

8.   Adam Enfroy. (n.d.). Strategies for maximizing affiliate marketing income using AI tools. Retrieved from https://www.adamenfroy.com

9.   Scaleo. (n.d.). An AI-powered affiliate marketing platform. Retrieved from https://www.scaleo.io

10.   Pepper Content. (n.d.). The benefits of AI in affiliate marketing. Retrieved from https://www.peppercontent.io

11.   ContentStudio Blog. (n.d.). Retrieved from https://blog.contentstudio.io

12.   Wirestock Blog. (n.d.). Retrieved from https://blog.wirestock.io

13.   Mighty Networks. (n.d.). Retrieved from https://www.mightynetworks.com

Chapter 4

1.   Influencer Marketing Hub. (2024). *Top 27 AI Marketing Tools to Grow Your Business in 2024*. Retrieved from https://www.influencermarketinghub.com/ai-marketing-tools/

2.   Hootsuite Blog. (2024). *25 AI Marketing Tools To Help You Win in 2024*. Retrieved from https://blog.hootsuite.com/ai-marketing-tools/

3.   Smart Insights. (2023-2024). *Trends in using AI for marketing: 2023-2024*. Retrieved from https://www.smartinsights.com/digital-marketing-strategy/ai-marketing-trends/

4.   Oneflow. (2024). *10 AI marketing tools you must try in 2024*. Retrieved from https://www.oneflow.com/ai-marketing-tools/

5.   Customerly. (n.d.). Retrieved from https://www.customerly.io/

6.   BCG. (n.d.). Retrieved from https://www.bcg.com/

7.   Dotdigital. (n.d.). Retrieved from https://www.dotdigital.com/

8.   Sensika. (n.d.). Retrieved from https://www.sensika.com/

9.   Customers.ai. (2024). *Top AI Tools for Businesses in 2024*. Retrieved from [Assumed URL based on the context, as no specific URL is provided] https://www.customers.ai/

10.   ClickUp. (2024). *10 Best AI Content Creation Tools for Content Marketing in 2024*. Retrieved from https://clickup.com/blog/ai-content-creation-tools/

11. Hootsuite Blog. (2024). *10 AI Content Creation Tools That Will Make Your Job Easier.* Retrieved from https://blog.hootsuite.com/ai-content-creation-tools/

12. ClickUp. (2024). *15 Best AI Content Generators & Tools to try in 2024 (Free & Paid).* Retrieved from https://clickup.com/blog/ai-content-generator/

13. Neil Chase Film. (2024). *The 9+ Best AI Content Creation Tools for Creatives in 2024.* Retrieved from https://neilchasefilm.com/ai-content-creation-tools/

14. Kajabi. (2024). *12 Best AI Content Creation Tools in 2024.* Retrieved from https://kajabi.com/blog/best-ai-content-creation-tools

15. Semrush. (n.d.). Retrieved from https://www.semrush.com/

16. Outranking. (n.d.). Retrieved from https://www.outranking.io/

17. Alli AI. (n.d.). Retrieved from https://www.alliai.com/

18. SE Ranking. (n.d.). Retrieved from https://seranking.com/

19. GrowthBar. (n.d.). Retrieved from https://www.growthbarseo.com/

20. FeedHive. (n.d.). Retrieved from https://feedhive.io/

21. Vista Social. (n.d.). Retrieved from https://www.vistasocial.com/

22. Buffer. (n.d.). Retrieved from https://buffer.com/

23. Flick. (n.d.). Retrieved from https://www.flick.tech/

24. Audiense. (n.d.). Retrieved from https://audiense.com/

25. Ocoya. (n.d.). Retrieved from https://www.ocoya.com/

26. Predis.ai. (n.d.). Retrieved from https://www.predis.ai/

27. ClickUp AI. (n.d.). Retrieved from https://clickup.com/

28. SocialBee. (n.d.). Retrieved from https://socialbee.io/

29. Hootsuite Blog. (2024). *The 15 Best AI Tools for Social Media in 2024.* Retrieved from https://blog.hootsuite.com/ai-tools-social-media/

30. SocialPilot. (2024). *10 Awesome Social Media AI Tools in 2024.* Retrieved from https://www.socialpilot.co/blog/social-media-ai-tools

31. Zapier. (2024). *The 12 Best AI Tools for Social Media Management in 2024.* Retrieved from https://zapier.com/blog/ai-social-media-management/

32. ClickUp Blog. (2024). *10 Best Social Media AI Tools for Social Media Managers in 2024.* Retrieved from https://clickup.com/blog/social-media-ai-tools/

33. ActiveCampaign. (n.d.). Retrieved from https://www.activecampaign.com/

34. Mailchimp. (n.d.). Retrieved from https://mailchimp.com/

35. Campaign Monitor. (n.d.). Retrieved from https://www.campaignmonitor.com/

36. Sendinblue. (n.d.). Retrieved from https://www.sendinblue.com/

37. Moosend. (n.d.). Retrieved from https://moosend.com/

38. Ultimate AI. (n.d.). Retrieved from https://www.ultimate.ai/

39. Zendesk. (n.d.). Retrieved from https://www.zendesk.com/

40. Freddy AI. (n.d.). *15 Best AI Chatbots for Customer Support.* Freddy AI is designed by CRM platform Freshworks to provide instant, automated solutions to common queries in multiple languages. Further information is available at Freshdesk. Retrieved from https://www.freshworks.com/ai-customer-support/

41. Bitrix24. (n.d.). *10 Best AI Chatbots For Customer Service in 2024.* Bitrix24 is highlighted for its CRM integration and communication tools. More information can be found at Bitrix24. Retrieved from https://www.bitrix24.com/

42. Intercom. (n.d.). *10 Best AI Chatbots For Customer Service in 2024.* Intercom offers

dependable functionality for efficient customer engagement. Discover more at Intercom. Retrieved from https://www.intercom.com/

43. Dixa. (n.d.). *10 Best AI Chatbots For Customer Service in 2024*. Dixa is noted for its conversational customer service platform. Learn more about Dixa at Dixa. Retrieved from https://www.dixa.com/

44. Salesforce. (n.d.). *10 Best AI Chatbots For Customer Service in 2024*. Salesforce provides integration between chatbots and CRM systems. More information is available at Salesforce. Retrieved from https://www.salesforce.com/

45. Smartwriter. (n.d.). Offers features for crafting personalized outreach emails and integrates with email marketing tools. More information on Smartwriter can be found at ClickUp's analysis. Retrieved from https://www.clickup.com/

46. Cohesive. (n.d.). Analyzes trends in competitors' content and offers a text-to-image generator. Insights on Cohesive available through ClickUp's analysis. Retrieved from https://www.clickup.com/

47. Semrush. (n.d.). Provides comprehensive analytics on competitors' online presence and marketing strategies. Retrieved from https://www.semrush.com/

48. Kompyte. (n.d.). Delivers real-time competitor updates and AI-driven analytics for strategic insights. Detailed analysis available via ClickUp. Retrieved from https://www.clickup.com/

49. Exploding Topics. (n.d.). Tracks trending topics and social listening for identifying market opportunities. Retrieved from https://explodingtopics.com/

Chapter 5

1. OpenAI. (2024). *DALL·E 3: Advanced AI for Image Generation*. Retrieved from https://openai.com/dall-e-3

2. Stability AI. (2024). *DreamStudio by Stable Diffusion*. Retrieved from https://dreamstudio.ai

3. Midjourney. (2024). *Midjourney: Innovative AI Art Generation*. Retrieved from https://www.midjourney.com

4. Canva. (2024). *Canva's AI Art Generator*. Retrieved from https://www.canva.com/features/ai-art-generator

5. NightCafe. (2024). *NightCafe: AI Art Generator*. Retrieved from https://creator.nightcafe.studio

6. OpenArt. (2024). *OpenArt: Enhance Your Creative Process with AI*. Retrieved from https://openart.ai

7. Adobe. (2024). *Adobe Firefly: AI Art Generator*. Retrieved from https://firefly.adobe.com

8. Jasper. (2024). *Jasper Art: AI-Driven Creativity*. Retrieved from https://www.jasper.ai/art

9. Zapier. (2024). The top AI art generators in 2024. Retrieved from https://zapier.com/blog/best-ai-art-generators/

10. AIArtists.org. (2021). Top 41 AI Art Generators: Make AI Art, Paintings & More. Retrieved from https://aiartists.org/ai-art-generators

11. Design Shack. (2024). 10 Best AI Art Generators & Tools in 2024. Retrieved from https://designshack.net/articles/inspiration/ai-art-generators/

12. Skyline Social. (n.d.). 17+ Best AI Image Generator 'Text to Art' Tools with Examples. Retrieved from https://www.skylinesocial.com/best-ai-image-generator-tools

13. For Unite.AI's "10 Best AI Graphic Design Tools (March 2024)", you can visit the Unite. Retrieved from https://unite.ai/

14. Chris Starkhagen's "7+ Best AI Graphic Design Tools In 2023 (Easy And Useful)". Retrieved from https://chrisstarkhagen.com/business/software/ai-graphic-design

15. For CareerFoundry's "The 10 Best AI Graphic Design Tools", Retrieved from https://careerfoundry.com

16. Create and Go. (2024). 16 Best AI Writing Tools In 2024 (Free And Paid). Retrieved from https://createandgo.com/best-ai-writing-tools/

17. ClickUp. (2024). 13 Best AI Writing Tools for Content Writing in 2024. Retrieved from https://clickup.com/blog/ai-writing-tools/

18. Unite.AI. (2024). 10 "Best" AI Writing Generators (March 2024). Retrieved from https://www.unite.ai/

19. Elegant Themes. (2024). 5 Best AI Music Generators in 2024 (Compared). Retrieved from https://www.elegantthemes.com/blog/marketing/best-ai-music-generators

20. EDM Sauce. (2024). The 7 Best AI Music Composers in 2024. Retrieved from https://www.edmsauce.com/best-ai-music-composers-2024/

21. Skyline Social. (n.d.). 10 Best AI Music Generator Tools for YouTube Content Creators. Retrieved from https://www.skylinesocial.com/best-ai-music-generator-tools

22. Adobe. (n.d.). Adobe Photoshop. Retrieved from https://www.adobe.com/products/photoshop.html

23. Skylum. (n.d.). Luminar Neo. Retrieved from https://skylum.com/luminar-neo

24. Kaleido AI GmbH. (n.d.). Remove.bg. Retrieved from https://www.remove.bg/

25. DeepArt. (n.d.). DeepArt.io. Retrieved from https://deepart.io/

26. Topaz Labs. (n.d.). Topaz Labs AI Tools. Retrieved from https://www.topazlabs.com/

27. Unite.AI. (2024). 10 Best AI Game Generators (March 2024). Retrieved from https://unite.ai/10-best-ai-game-generators-march-2024/

28. European Gaming Industry News. (n.d.). Five AI tools every game developer should have in their toolbelt. Retrieved from https://europeangaming.eu/portal/latest-news/2024/03/05/five-ai-tools-every-game-developer-should-have-in-their-toolbelt/

29. Unity Technologies. (n.d.). Unity AI - Create Incredible Experiences with Real-Time 3D. Retrieved from https://unity.com/products/unity-ai

30. Toolify. (n.d.). Create realistic AI influencers: Instagram and OnlyFans models. Retrieved from https://www.toolify.ai

31. Toolify. (n.d.). Make money with your own AI influencer. Retrieved from https://www.toolify.ai

32. CUT THE SAAS. (n.d.). Retrieved from https://www.cut-the-saas.com

33. 34th Street Magazine. (n.d.). Retrieved from https://www.34st.com

34. HubSpot Blog. (n.d.). Retrieved from https://blog.hubspot.com

35. Mubert. (n.d.). An in-depth study into AI music: Its creators, composers, and adopters. Mubert. Retrieved March 13, 2024, from https://mubert.com/blog/an-in-depth-study-into-ai-music-its-creators-composers-and-adopters

36. Whiddington, R. (2023, April 21). Damien Hirst's New A.I. Project, Which Asked Collectors to Generate Their Own Paintings, Earned Him $20 Million in Nine Days.

Artnet News. https://news.artnet.com/market/hirst-beautiful-paintings-sale-20-million-9-days-2289386

37. Christie's. (n.d.). What I have learned: Nicole Sales Giles on digital art. Christie's. https://www.christies.com/en/stories/what-i-have-learned-nicole-sales-giles-digital-art-b0e99335210b4d5b946c6895309fc0e0

Chapter 6

1. HousingWire. (2023). "24 AI tools to revamp your real estate business in 2024." Retrieved from https://www.housingwire.com/articles/24-ai-tools-to-revamp-your-real-estate-business-in-2024/
2. Built In. (n.d.). "AI in Real Estate: 21 Examples to Know." Retrieved from https://builtin.com/real-estate-technology/ai-in-real-estate
3. The Close. (n.d.). "Real Estate AI: 20 Mind-blowing Artificial Intelligence Tools." Retrieved from https://theclose.com/real-estate-ai/
4. ClickUp. (2024). "10 Educational AI Tools for Students in 2024." Retrieved from https://clickup.com/blog/ai-education-tools-2024/
5. Unite.AI. (2024). "10 Best AI Tools for Education (March 2024)." Retrieved from https://www.unite.ai/10-best-ai-tools-for-education-march-2024/
6. Analytics Insight. (2023). "Top 10 AI Tools for Education in 2023." Retrieved from https://www.analyticsinsight.net/top-10-ai-tools-for-education-in-2023/
7. HealthTech Magazine. (2023). "AI in Healthcare, Where It's Going in 2023: ML, NLP & More." Retrieved from https://healthtechmagazine.net/sections/healthcare-it/ai-healthcare-where-its-going-2023-ml-nlp-more
8. StartUs Insights. (2023). "Top 10 AI Trends in Healthcare (2023)." Retrieved from https://www.startus-insights.com/innovators-guide/top-10-ai-trends-in-healthcare-to-watch-in-2023/
9. McKinsey. (2023). "Generative AI in healthcare: Emerging use for care." Retrieved from https://www.mckinsey.com/industries/healthcare-systems-and-services/our-insights/generative-ai-in-healthcare-emerging-use-for-care
10. World Economic Forum. (2023). "Emerging tech like AI are poised to make healthcare more accurate, accessible, and sustainable." Retrieved from https://www.weforum.org/agenda/2023/06/emerging-tech-like-ai-are-poised-to-make-healthcare-more-accurate-accessible-and-sustainable/
11. WiserAdvisor. (n.d.). "Can You Use AI For Effective Money Management." Retrieved from https://www.wiseradvisor.com/
12. Finance Magnates. (2023). "How AI is Revolutionizing Personal Finance in 2023." Retrieved from https://www.financemagnates.com/fintech/news/how-ai-is-revolutionizing-personal-finance-in-2023/
13. Deloitte. (n.d.). "The Impact of Generative AI in Finance." Retrieved from https://www2.deloitte.com/us/en/pages/financial-services/articles/generative-ai-in-finance.html
14. MoneyFit. (n.d.). "The AI Revolution in Personal Finance: A Forecast." Retrieved from https://www.moneyfit.org/blog/the-ai-revolution-in-personal-finance-a-forecast
15. V7 Labs. (2023). *AI in Agriculture: 8 Practical Applications [2023 Update].* Retrieved from https://www.v7labs.com/blog/ai-in-agriculture

16. Intellias. (n.d.). *AI in Agriculture: Challenges, Benefits, and Use Cases*. Retrieved from https://www.intellias.com/how-ai-is-transforming-agriculture

17. Harvard International Review. (n.d.). *The Future of Farming: Artificial Intelligence and Agriculture*. Retrieved from https://hir.harvard.edu/the-future-of-farming-artificial-intelligence-and-agriculture/

18. Texas A&M Today. (n.d.). *Texas A&M Researchers Integrating New AI Tools For Plant Analysis*. Retrieved from https://today.tamu.edu/2023/05/03/texas-am-researchers-integrating-new-ai-tools-for-plant-analysis/

19. MarketsandMarkets. (n.d.). *Artificial Intelligence in Agriculture Market Size, Industry Research Report, Trends and Growth Drivers - 2032*. Retrieved from https://www.marketsandmarkets.com/Market-Reports/artificial-intelligence-in-agriculture-market-159957009.html

20. SME. (n.d.). *AI Enables What's Next in Manufacturing*. Retrieved from https://www.sme.org/technologies/articles/2021/march/ai-enables-whats-next-in-manufacturing/

21. Microsoft. (n.d.). *AI in Manufacturing: Solutions & Stories*. Retrieved from https://www.microsoft.com/en-us/ai/ai-in-manufacturing

22. Murf. (n.d.). *Top 7 Applications of AI in Manufacturing Industry*. Retrieved from https://murf.ai/blog/applications-of-ai-in-manufacturing-industry

23. ClickUp. (n.d.). *10 AI Tools for Manufacturing Teams and Projects in 2024*. Retrieved from https://clickup.com/blog/ai-tools-manufacturing/

24. Intellias. (n.d.). *AI in Supply Chain: Challenges, Benefits, & Use Cases*. Retrieved from https://www.intellias.com/success-stories/ai-in-supply-chain/

25. Built In. (n.d.). *17 Examples of AI in Supply Chain and Logistics*. Retrieved from https://builtin.com/artificial-intelligence/ai-in-logistics-supply-chain

26. IBM Blog. (n.d.). *How generative AI is revolutionizing supply chain operations*. Retrieved from https://www.ibm.com/blogs/journey-to-ai/2021/05/how-generative-ai-is-revolutionizing-supply-chain-operations/

27. DHL Freight Connections. (n.d.). *Logistics Trends 2023/2024: Which Direction for AI?* Retrieved from https://dhl-freight-connections.com/en/logistics-trends-2023-2024-which-direction-for-ai/

Chapter 7

1. Google Ads. (n.d.). *Keyword Planner*. Retrieved from https://ads.google.com/home/tools/keyword-planner/

2. CB Insights. (n.d.). Retrieved from https://www.cbinsights.com/

3. TechCrunch. (n.d.). Retrieved from https://techcrunch.com/

4. Google Cloud. (n.d.). Retrieved from https://cloud.google.com

5. Amazon Web Services. (n.d.). Retrieved from https://aws.amazon.com

6. Microsoft AI. (n.d.). Retrieved from https://www.microsoft.com/en-us/ai

7. Project Management. (n.d.). Retrieved from https://www.projectmanagement.com

8. Brownlee, J. (n.d.). *Your First Machine Learning Project in Python Step-By-Step*. Machine Learning Mastery. Retrieved from https://machinelearningmastery.com/your-first-machine-learning-project-in-python-step-by-step/

9. Brownlee, J. (n.d.). *Your First Deep Learning Project in Python With Keras Step-By-Step.*

Machine Learning Mastery. Retrieved from https://machinelearningmastery.com/your-first-deep-learning-project-in-python-with-keras-step-by-step/

10. Plat.AI. (n.d.). *How to Build an AI*. Retrieved from https://plat.ai/

11. The Code Dose. (n.d.). *Creating Your First AI Chatbot Using Python*. Retrieved from https://thecodedose.com/

12. Elegant Themes. (n.d.). *Making Your Own AI*. Retrieved from https://www.elegantthemes.com/blog/

13. TensorFlow. (n.d.). Retrieved from https://www.tensorflow.org

14. Scikit-learn. (n.d.). Retrieved from https://scikit-learn.org

15. PyTorch. (n.d.). Retrieved from https://www.pytorch.org

16. Keras. (n.d.). Retrieved from https://keras.io

17. OpenCV. (n.d.). Retrieved from https://opencv.org

18. Code Intelligence. (n.d.). *Top 18 AI-Powered Software Testing Tools in 2024*. Retrieved from https://www.code-intelligence.com/blog/ai-powered-software-testing-tools

19. TestingXperts. (n.d.). *AI in Software Testing | Best Approaches to Look in 2024*. Retrieved from https://www.testingxperts.com/blog/ai-in-software-testing

20. Neptune.ai. (n.d.). *5 Tools That Will Help You Setup Production ML Model Testing*. Retrieved from https://neptune.ai/blog/production-ml-model-testing-tools

21. Testsigma. (n.d.). *AI Testing Tools*. Retrieved from https://testsigma.com/tools/ai-testing-tools/

22. Fireflies.ai. (n.d.). Retrieved from https://fireflies.ai/

23. Midjourney. (n.d.). Retrieved from https://midjourney.com/

24. DALL-E 2 by OpenAI. (n.d.). Retrieved from https://openai.com/dall-e-2/

25. Tome. (n.d.). Retrieved from https://tome.app/

26. Lumen5. (n.d.). Retrieved from https://lumen5.com/

27. Sharma, A. (2024). *25 Best ChatGPT Chrome Extensions*. Beebom. Retrieved from https://beebom.com/best-chatgpt-chrome-extensions/

28. Southern, M. (2023). *22 Of The Best ChatGPT Chrome Extensions To Try*. Search Engine Journal. Retrieved from https://www.searchenginejournal.com/best-chatgpt-chrome-extensions/

www.ingramcontent.com/pod-product-compliance
Lightning Source LLC
Chambersburg PA
CBHW021656070726
47591CB00017B/548